GREG NORMAN
MY STORY

GREG NORMAN

MY STORY

By Greg Norman
with Don Lawrence

Foreword by
Peter Alliss

HARRAP  LONDON

I would like to dedicate this book to
my father Mervyn, my mother Toini and
my wife Laura for all the assistance
they gave me in compiling it.

And to John Klatt and Charlie Earp,
the two wonderful professional golfers
who started it all.

First published in Great Britain 1983
by HARRAP LIMITED
19-23 Ludgate Hill, London EC4M 7PD

© *Eulbertie Ltd* 1983

ISBN 0 245-53923-9

Designed by Michael R. Carter

Printed and bound in Great Britain
by R. J. Acford, Chichester

CONTENTS

FOREWORD
by Peter Alliss

When I look back on my life in golf I quickly realize how fortunate I have been in seeing the earliest beginnings of many of the world's greatest golfers: Peter Thomson, Gary Player, Arnold Palmer, Jack Nicklaus, Tom Watson and Seve Ballesteros to name but a few.

I feel I'm a 'good spotter' of a potential 'star' — they have a certain air about them that's hard to explain. It is a quiet arrogance, a look in the eyes — the desire to be great is there for all to see. It fair makes your heart beat faster. I felt that when I first saw Greg Norman. Greg was in fact a late starter, not taking up the game until his late teens, using his mother's clubs. Mum soon spotted her son's obvious talent, and he got a set of clubs all to himself. Within two years he was playing to scratch, at twenty-one he won his first important event, the West Lakes Classic in Adelaide — the year 1976. The field included David Graham, Graham Marsh, Bruce Devlin, Bruce Crampton and Bob Shearer. People sat up and took notice. He hit the ball miles, and straight. He had a lean, athletic body, toned down by years of surfing and exercise. His startling blond hair and his granite-like good looks all helped to create 'the image'.

Greg Norman has been blessed with a great deal of talent; he works at his game as hard as anyone in the world of golf. He is very conscious that he has yet to win one of the world's four 'majors', but all of them are within his reach, including the Open, once he fully masters the art of playing the British seaside links, of mastering the wind, the bounce, the pitch-and-run shot, the unfairness at times of it all. He has already proved that those huge drives and high-flying iron shots are made for American target golf.

Greg Norman *will* be a world star of the 1980s; his name *will* rank with those others I saw step out on the road to fame and fortune.

The desire and the skill already is at his disposal. In 1982 he was the first Australian to win the Vardon Trophy since Norman Von Nida in 1947. He is a past winner of the World Match Play Championship and two Dunlop Masters but all the victories and wealth that have come his way in the past six years are but an apéritif to the main banquet that cannot be far away.

CHAPTER 1
COMING OF AGE

I am not a man who looks over his shoulder at the path his life has taken, but when Jack Nicklaus said to me, 'Take a deep breath and let's enjoy the golf' I felt entitled to the memories.

Jack's brief remark was just what I would expect from him. It was warm and friendly and aimed at easing any tension I might have felt as we left the first tee at Augusta, Georgia, both seeking victory in the U.S. Masters and both in a position to achieve it. The year was 1981, and for me a momentous one. I was playing in my very first U.S. Masters, and alongside me was a man who had already worn the prized green jacket five times, and was seeking it for an unprecedented sixth, a man who rates among the all-time greats of golf.

Augusta was bursting forth in all its flowered beauty, and the thousands of fans who crammed the gallery ropes were there to watch the mighty Golden Bear in action. In their minds I was the 'bit' player, Jack Nicklaus's partner, the kid from Australia with the blond hair who had caused a ripple or two in the opening half of the tournament but probably wouldn't be around much longer. I felt well content with my opening tee shot of that crucial third round, and as we strode towards our second shots I said to myself, 'That was nice of Jack to say that.'

And then I blotted out everything except for the task ahead. This was a moment I had dreamed of for years. I was not here by accident. I had earned my place alongside Nicklaus, and to hell with what they were whispering in the galleries and the Press tent.

Playing alongside Nicklaus on that excitement-packed, crowded third day at Augusta, I could not resist a quick flashback to my rookie year in professional golf in my native Australia.

In only my fourth tournament on the tour I had got it all together in the West Lakes Classic in Adelaide to score a five-shot victory over a field which included David Graham, Bruce Crampton, Graham Marsh, Bob Shearer and Jack Newton. It was a dream introduction to the pro life as I raced to a five-shot win and finished 13 under par. I was just twenty-one years old, and the reward for my scoring splurge in Adelaide was to be drawn alongside the Golden Bear for the first two rounds of the Australian Open in Sydney the following week.

At the time of my Adelaide success I was still a trainee professional, and could only compete in tournaments by invitation. However, my win had attracted

Opposite
Happy Birthday from the 1983 Victorian Open Championship in Australia. But not so happy when I bogeyed the last two holes and ran second to Bob Shearer.

9

enormous publicity, through both the Press and television, and now I was classified as something of a sensation. But I felt like a sacrificial lamb. The draw was flattering, but I knew I had been thrown to the wolves by a tournament organization eager to capitalize on the already publicized physical resemblance between the great Golden Bear and myself. I learned of my draw several days before the tournament started, and with just a few tournaments behind me the thought of standing up alongside Jack Nicklaus was daunting indeed. I had mixed feelings. I was overjoyed at the chance, but apprehensive too.

I spotted Jack several times before the first day of the tournament as we practised around The Australian layout, but the first time I actually met him was the day before the tournament started. Then I stood shyly beside him while photographers hungrily took the bait that the Australian Golf Union had set, and our next meeting was on the first tee. There was a huge crowd there to watch Jack, and when my turn to tee off came the butterflies in my stomach were in full flight. I 'cold topped' my opening drive about 30 yards, catching a tree just in front of the elevated tee.

I took 80 that day, while Jack fired 72. I was embarrassed. I hardly spoke a word. I was angry and disappointed with myself for playing the way I did, not only in front of Nicklaus but in front of all those people. I knew he could sense my disappointment, and I appreciated the few words he spoke to me, but as bogey followed bogey he understood there was little consolation in anything he could say.

I went back to my hotel that night and slept on the anguish of the day, determined that I would make amends in tomorrow's second round. My pride was repaired with a par equalling 72, two shots better than Jack Nicklaus, and when he invited me for a chat in the locker-room after the round my cup 'runneth over.' Our lockers were virtually next door to each other, as they had been allocated alphabetically. I followed him into the locker bay, and we sat down beside each other while he talked of my potential and the chances that lay ahead of me if I would go to America.

That chat with the Great Man was worth all the trauma I had been through the day before. I was overjoyed that he had taken the time to offer me encouragement. For twenty minutes we sat and talked, and it is twenty minutes of my life I will never forget. I would have loved to have told him right there how the first book I ever read on golf he had written. How I used to sneak it into the classroom at High School in Brisbane and practise my grip under the desk. But I just sat and listened. I was too shy to say much. One day I must tell him about that golf book. I have got to know him better.

And now just a short five years later I was at Augusta, alongside Jack Nicklaus, in contention and determined to 'hang around' for a lot longer than most people believed I could.

In the intervening years since that Sydney embarrassment a lot of things had happened to Greg Norman. They had happened at a breath-taking pace, and tournament victories across the world had pushed into a fading memory that feeling of inferiority and inadequacy I had felt on the first tee in Sydney.

Now I felt I was there as an equal.

Jack and I were the last pair to tee off on that third day at Augusta, and I fired an even par 72 and watched Jack's score soar to 75 as he surrendered the lead to Tom Watson with a round to go.

Opposite
With Jack Nicklaus at Augusta in 1981. It was my first U.S. Masters and I finished fourth.

10

Jack had gone into the third day leading the tournament by four shots at the halfway mark ahead of myself, Watson and Bruce Lietzke, all on 5 under par, with Jack setting a scorching pace at 9 under after openers of 70, 65. But on Saturday Jack had his troubles. Very few things happened the way he wanted them to, yet through the long afternoon I did not miss the little niceties that came from him. Every time I made a birdie he stood back and let me walk to the next tee ahead of him. Among that roaring, partisan crowd Nicklaus made certain I was not going to be run over. They roared for Jack, climbed the peaks and descended the troughs with their old favourite, but as he vainly sought his sixth Masters title Jack Nicklaus did not forget he had a playing partner.

I was content with my opening scores of 69, 70, but would have been more so if I had not bogeyed the last hole on both those opening days. After a third-round 72 only Watson on 209 (71, 68, 70) and Nicklaus 210 (70, 65, 75) were ahead of me, and I was just two shots away from the lead. Next day I played alongside Watson, again in the final group, and again surprising everybody just by being there. For the second day in a row I returned an even par score of 72, and emerged from a tremendous struggle for the title in fourth place behind the winner Tom Watson and Nicklaus and Johnny Miller, who had tied for second just a shot in front of me on 6 under par.

That was my introduction to Augusta, and when I returned to the house my manager James Marshall and I were sharing a few miles from the course it was with a feeling of happy disappointment. I really felt that I could have won the tournament, because I believed I had played the most consistent golf of anybody over those four exhilarating days. I relished the pressure, and I fell in love with Augusta and its generous fairways and slick greens. It was not my first experience of golf in the United States, where I believe tournament organizers — and galleries too — better understand and appreciate the professional golfer than in any other country on earth. But up to now it is certainly my happiest American experience.

After the final round at Augusta I felt exhausted. That is the barometer that tells me at the end of a tournament that I have given it my best shot. When I am mentally and physically weary I have done my best. If I get back to the house or hotel after a tournament and feel like stepping out, then I have given myself the message that I could have done better. I felt I had developed an empathy with Augusta and what it stood for, and was more than anxious for another taste of the same.

Playing with Watson on the closing day was an entirely different sort of experience to my previous day with Nicklaus. He could not have spoken five words in the entire round, and I felt that he was hardly aware that I was there. However, I dare say he figured me as a rival, just as threatening to his winning hopes as Jack Nicklaus or anybody else. The only time we exchanged words was in the scorers' tent at the end of the round, when we shook hands and I congratulated him on his success.

I had never experienced anything approaching the pressure-cooker atmosphere of that final day at Augusta, where the magnificent stage veiled only thinly the turmoil inside competitors and spectators alike.

When Watson bogeyed the 9th hole and I turned in level par figures just one shot separated me from the lead, and that narrowest of margins came about when Watson's first putt slipped uncontrollably off the green. He chipped it

back with a sand iron, and was forced to hole from 8 feet to save his bogey.

It was at the next hole that I made the error that probably cost me the tournament. Perhaps I was too anxious to get my tee shot away. Watson's bogey had set the crowd alight, and as we pushed our way through the excited, noisy fans I should have told myself to slow down.

I didn't. I know I rushed my tee shot, although when I made contact and watched the ball fly close to the left-hand treeline I really believed it would be safe. Nevertheless, the gods of golf dictated otherwise, and when I got to it the ball had kicked cruelly into trouble, and I finally came up with a double bogey 6.

I set out to patch up the damage, and it was really the birdie chances that I missed at the next two holes that took the edge off my winning chances.

I missed from a bare 6 feet at the 11th, and less than that at the 12th. At the long 13th I pummelled a 5 iron 18 feet below the hole, and there was an eagle there for the taking, but the ball died away from the hole at the last second.

Congratulating Tom Watson after he had won the 1981 U.S. Masters at Augusta.

13

I made another birdie at the 15th, but Watson matched it, and I was still running two shots behind with Nicklaus just one ahead and Johnny Miller bursting on to the scene. Miller's final round of 68 lifted him into a tie for second with Jack, and pushed me back to fourth.

If I had achieved nothing else, I believe I had justified the invitation to play, an invitation that had arrived at my parents' home in the Brisbane suburb of Aspley several months before, and set me on course to achieving one of my prime ambitions in golf. Just to play in the U.S. Masters was a milestone, but to perform so well was reaching into fairytale land.

Playing in the final group on the last two days had also pushed me in front of the biggest television golf audience in the world. I had arrived at Augusta several days early, to practise and familiarize myself with this Mecca of golf, and was amused when I read one article in the Press describing me as an 'Australian amateur'. I hope the author realizes his mistake, which was certainly not one that the media army at Augusta repeated. However, I feel that now is the right time to explain away a slight misunderstanding I had with them all.

After my first round I was ushered into the Press area for the sort of grilling that goes along with a new face and a score that shares the lead. As *Golf Digest* correspondent Dwayne Netland wrote, 'Over the last few years we had heard bits and pieces about him — that he was an extremely long hitter from Australia with an impressive record in Europe. But hardly any of us, except a handful of American spectators and touring pros, had actually seen him play until he teed up at this year's Masters and finished an astonishing fourth.'

Well, one thing led to another during my talks with the Press guys, and somehow they got the notion that I used to shoot sharks as a hobby, and within a twinkling I was tagged 'The Great White Shark'. After my first-day 69 they were thirsting for information on my background, my life-style and anything else that could help them introduce this young Australian to their readers. I told them I hated sharks and would love to shoot them, and that is where the misunderstanding started, because the next thing I knew I had my new label.

It was true that I had caught many sharks beach-fishing off the coast of Queensland and up around the Great Barrier Reef, but as for shooting a shark — never. Many was the time I would have dearly loved a rifle to take a shot at those marauders as they fed from the fish I caught.

When I got back to Australia later that year I decided to put my conscience at ease. I owned a 28-foot ocean-going cruiser moored at the jetty outside the backdoor of my Paradise Point home on the Queensland Gold Coast. I carefully stored a .303 rifle in the cabin, with several ammunition clips. For several hours I cruised along the coast until I eventually spotted the tell-tale dorsal fin of a cruising shark. I buried several bullets into the thick skin of an ugly hammerhead, and hoped those American golf-writers understood. However, the 1981 Masters did more than introduce me to the American sporting public. On that final night I asked my American girl friend Laura Andrassy if she would marry me. She accepted.

CHAPTER 2
TOWNSVILLE DAYS

Magnetic Island nestles just a few miles off the North Queensland coastal town of Townsville, and for years it has been the haven of sun-seekers from Australia's cooler southern cities. It is now a well-commercialized holiday resort, with its waving tropical palms and white sands lapped by the blue waters of the Pacific Ocean.

I was born in the outback mining town of Mt Isa on 10 February 1955, and was only a baby when my father Merv and mother Toini decided to move to the coast. Townsville was where they settled.

For the next fifteen years Magnetic Island was a playground for the Norman family. It was almost at our back door, and we spent hundreds of happy days there exploiting its tropical charm and idyllic setting at every opportunity. It was a wonderful part of the world for any youngster to grow up. They were my barefoot days — happy, lazy days where what happened outside Townsville and Magnetic Island could have happened on another planet for all I cared.

Until a cyclone flattened it to the ground, my parents owned a simple shack on Magnetic Island, and in holiday-time we used it as our base as we explored the underwater beauty of the coral reefs and speared fresh fish. My sister Janis and I spent many hours under water stalking our prey, and would then bring the fish home in triumph, where my mother would cook them over an open fire.

My father had been employed by the giant Mt Isa Mining company, but elected to branch out in the engineering business on his own account, and shortly after the family arrived in Townsville he started in private practice as a professional engineer.

Both my parents had been active in Mt Isa's restricted sporting world, playing both golf and tennis at the local clubs, and it is fair to say that I was going around a golf course before I was born. Up to a month or two before I arrived my mother continued to play her weekly golf games around the sand greens at Mt Isa, but certainly without any pre-natal premonition that the baby she was carrying would one day take the game a little more seriously.

As a younger man, my father was an electrician with Mt Isa Mines, and when I took my wife Laura back to my birthplace recently for a 'golf day with Greg Norman' we were handed a sample of good old Aussie outback hospitality. We were taken on a conducted tour thousands of feet underground dressed in all the protective and safety gear the miners wear. I played an exhibition next day, and was 3 over par when a cloudburst thankfully ended it.

My parents' holiday home on Magnetic Island off the North Queensland coast, before it was flattened by a cyclone.

It was many years earlier that my father had played a leading role in bringing to the then new clubhouse the power lines that would carry the luxury of electric light to the members. The older members of Mt Isa Golf Club still remember the celebrations with a chuckle. 'Your Dad was a prankster', they told me, and because I had not heard the story I pressed them further.

And this is what happened when the Mt Isa Golf Club gathered the members together for the ceremonial switching on of the power. It had taken my father and a team of volunteers many week-ends of hard labour to erect the power lines and run them from the township the several miles to the golf-club. It had been back-breaking work, all done in their spare time. A sub-station had to be built, and was located about 100 yards from the clubhouse.

When it was all completed and tested, invitations went out for the 'switch-on' ceremony and they came from miles around to watch company general manager Mr Clem Gross press the red button that would turn on the lights. After making an appropriate speech Mr Gross leaned forward and pushed the button. For a few seconds the electric bulbs shed their light and then — WOOMF — a huge explosion shook the clubhouse and the lights went out.

Revisiting the Queensland
mining town of Mt Isa
where I was born. Laura
and I toured
underground.

Poor Mr Gross was certain he had fouled it up. What he did not know was that my father and his friends had hatched up a 'gunpowder plot' that would have made Guy Fawkes envious. Behind the sub-station, and out of sight from the clubhouse, they ran a line between two trees, and from it they suspended several sticks of gelignite. Hidden in the bushes a safe distance away knelt one of the conspirators with the detonating mechanism in his hand, ready to go into action the split-second the lights went on in the clubhouse. You might say he was the 'sound-effects' man. In the clubhouse itself was another of the conspirators, whose job it was to throw the main switch and turn off the lights when the explosion came.

It all went like clockwork. Mr Gross pressed the button, the lights went on, the gelignite exploded with a bang and the lights went out. While he was trying to work out how the simple act of pressing a button could cause all that pandemonium the conspirator in the clubhouse turned the lights back on. There were plenty of laughs as the party continued and the 'guilty' ones explained how they planned their little diversion!

Needless to say, Mt Isa Golf Club had good reason to remember Merv Norman and the day he organized its electric light.

I have many vivid memories of my childhood in Townsville, but unfortunately not many of them revolve around any academic achievements.

To say I disliked school would about sum up my approach to the world of learning. My mind was always wandering to the beach, or to the horses I used to ride, or to the little Sabot sailing-boat my father had built Janis and me. My free spirit never did come to terms with the confines of the classroom, yet I managed to scramble through each term examination with a pass. If I had any good subjects they were geography and technical drawing. I hated French. I could not handle it at all.

Perhaps it was my lack of application that turned me away from my studies, but more likely it was the lure of the outdoor life and everything that tropical Townsville had to offer. One day I hope to go back there. To see Peter Rawkins, Peter and David Hay, Myles Bailey and Adrian Erklens. While we were all growing up it was with them that I enjoyed many of my greatest adventures … and a setback or two. Peter Rawkins was a keen horseback rider, and I shared that enthusiasm with him. He owned an old gelding fondly named Big Red, and we used to keep our horses in a paddock (field) at the back of our home. A high wire fence surrounded the paddock, and every time we decided to throw a bridle on the horses we would have to ride our bicycles some three miles around to the main gate of the compound, catch them and then lead them home before setting off.

It was a long process. One day I decided there was an easier way. I obtained a pair of wire-cutters, and in a few minutes cut a hole in the fence big enough to squeeze through. In a twinkling I had the bridle on my horse, and rode out through the main gate. But the council ranger had spotted me in the act, and from that day onward I had to find another paddock in which to graze my horse. He was an angry man as he banished me from that grassy paddock for ever, threatening to tell my parents of my misdeeds. The ranger's anger never did dampen my enthusiasm for riding, and some of my fondest memories of Townsville are of the days Peter and I spent galloping along the firm sands of the Queensland coastline. We always rode bareback. We could not afford saddles,

Opposite
A jet stream from a sandy lie during the 'Greg Norman day' at Mt Isa Golf Club.

19

and anyway they were a luxury to which we were not accustomed. With a cut lunch slung in a bag across our backs we would be away from sun-up to sun-down, covering more than twenty miles in a day's ride. It was exhilarating to give our mounts their heads and gallop along the beach with the wind singing in our hair and bringing tears to our eyes. At intervals we would walk the horses into the shallows, and Peter and I would tumble off their backs for a dip in the ocean, never forgetting to cling to the bridles.

I often wonder how life has treated Peter. He was a keen musician, and played the guitar. The last I heard of him he had started his own band, and one day I want to go back to Townsville and listen to him play again. Our rides were a week-end ritual that continued for a long time, and if we were not horseback riding together then we were skin-diving together around the coral reefs of Magnetic Island. Whenever we went riding my black labrador Pancho panted along at the heels of the horses, and I guess enjoyed the adventure as much as we did. My passion for riding horses might have led me into the life of a jackeroo but for my parents' subsequent decision to leave Townsville and move to Brisbane. During one school holiday period while we were still at Townsville my father arranged for me to spend several weeks on a cattle station in the outback, where I rode at the musters alongside the cattle hands who had been 'born to the saddle'. The station I went to was west of Charters Towers, and measured about 70 square miles — not large by Australian standards. I worked the stock with those old hands for several weeks, rounding up the strays and cutting out the cattle the owner wanted for slaughter. It was hard bush work, and I loved the chase, but any thoughts I had of a jackeroo's life ended when I found myself assigned to a team castrating bulls.

I was happy to get back to Townsville. There was great excitement in the Norman household when my father announced that he was going to build Janis and me a yacht. A close friend in Townsville, Bob Jones, provided us with the plans and for the next few months our backyard was like a mini Clydeside as we pored over them and finally got together our little Sabot. The Sabot class is purely for beginners, with no jib but simply a mainsail and tiller to worry about. Janis and I had joined the local Townsville sailing club and were eager to test ourselves under racing conditions.

But who was to be the skipper of our *Peter Pan*? Janis, two years older than me, insisted that she should take captaincy of our boat.

Although I finally won the argument Janis did not 'sink' without a real struggle. She turned out to be a very adept mainsheet hand, and when we sailed *Peter Pan* to victory in the B Grade club championship I was learning how to be a competitor.

But the victory came at a price. Janis left my 'crew' and did her sailing aboard another Sabot whose owner allowed her the privilege of being skipper. From then on I sailed *Peter Pan* by myself, handling tiller and mainsheet, but I was never to win another race, and perhaps Janis believed it was just reward for my chauvinism.

I hope *Peter Pan* is still sailing merrily along on the calm waters off Townsville. She gave us many hours of pleasure, and I would like to think she is keeping up the good work.

Life rolled on easily and comfortably, with the need to study occasionally punctuating an otherwise perfect outdoors existence.

Opposite
Going fishing with my sister Janis on Christmas Day 1962.

21

The crew of the *Peter Pan* prepare to set sail.

As for most kids in this part of the world, it was almost mandatory to play Rugby League football, and I was a handy lock forward in Townsville Grammar's line-up. On reflection I must have been a little better than 'handy' because I was selected to represent North Queensland against South-East Queensland, and it was a match I am unlikely to forget. I scored the only try for our team as we were comprehensively thrashed 48-3 by the opposition.

I was never over-keen about rugby, and after a couple of nasty injuries decided it was not a game I would pursue.

Dr Bob Hay, father of my school friends Peter and David Hay, owned an ocean-going cruiser, and during school holidays I was invited to go 'island-hopping' with them on trips that would take us to sea for weeks at a time. By day we would fish with a handline over the side or tip ourselves overboard and go searching for our prey with a speargun. By night we would anchor the *Tamana* in a sheltered cove at one of the scores of tiny coral islands in the Great Barrier Reef, wade ashore with our haul and cook our meal over a campfire. Many times I fell asleep under the stars, happily exhausted by the day's fishing and looking forward eagerly to tomorrow's adventures.

One day I was well below the surface searching for my evening meal when I sighted a healthy big fish, trained my speargun on it and pulled the trigger. I caught my quarry right amidships, but the velocity of the spearhead carried it several feet farther, and it embedded itself in a coral outcrop. I gave a tug but the spearhead refused to budge; several more tugs but nothing happened. While I was pondering how to remove the spearhead from the coral I glanced to my left, and through the bubbles I could see a shark approaching — and moving fast. It was six, perhaps seven, feet long, but it was not me it was after but the fish impaled halfway along the shaft of my speargun. I let everything drop and floated back to the surface, keeping a wary eye on the intruder in case he changed his mind. When I reached the surface I turned on my stomach and watched the shark through the glass visor of my underwater mask. A couple of healthy chomps and my catch had been gobbled up. I went back down, and finally wrenched my speargun from the coral and went searching for another fish.

We had several big hauls from the sea during these long expeditions, and would often return to Townsville with a commercial load.

One of our trips turned out to be disastrous for me.

At the stern of our cruiser there was a large hold where the fish were dumped

My tenth birthday party.

as we swung them inboard. It was called the killing pit, and I was making my way aft to help one late afternoon when I slipped and fell. It was an awkward tumble, and the result was that I broke my two front teeth on the edge of the killing pit. One of my teeth had snapped diagonally from the bottom tip up to the gum line. The other had broken horizontally half-way up the tooth.

The accident caused a great deal of consternation, and Dr Hay set a course for Townsville immediately so that I could see a dentist and find out just how serious was the damage. Over the next few years these teeth were to be a source of worry to myself and my family. I had a temporary capping in Townsville, and waited for several months to see if any permanent damage had been caused to the nerves.

Later I saw a specialist in Townsville and was given further temporary cappings, but it was not until I won the West Lakes Classic six years later that I finally had the job on my two front teeth completed properly.

By now I was nearly fifteen years old, and the Norman family days at Townsville were drawing to a close. My father decided to retire from his partnership in the well-established engineering company he had helped to found and to accept an offer to return to Mt Isa Mines, Ltd. He was to be stationed in Brisbane. But before we left Townsville there were several more family trips to Magnetic Island. It was late one Sunday afternoon when we had tired of swimming and fishing that my mother suggested we visit the island's nine-hole golf course. Her keenness for the game had never waned and in the years that we spent in Townsville she had been a regular player. I was preoccupied in too many other areas to think about this quaint pastime, but agreed to join her and my father for a few holes. My mother recalls that I had the basis of a reasonable swing, but all I can recall about my first golf outing was that I swiped lustily at one shot and the ball disappeared up a Pandamus Palm tree.

For all I know it could still be there.

CHAPTER 3
HOOKED ON GOLF

From the time I started to make my mark in tournament golf in the mid-seventies golf-writers around the world have found a flattering resemblance between myself and Jack Nicklaus.

It is a comparison based purely on a physical resemblance, and accentuated by the fact that we both own heads of blond hair. It is extraordinary the number of times I have been asked whether or not I dye my hair to maintain its colour, and to set the record straight I do not. Queensland's sun and surf have helped bleach it to the colour it is, but the real reason for my fair thatch is a genetic one.

My mother Toini is Finnish. Her parents Seth and Tyyne Hovi were married in Finland and migrated to Australia around 1930, and shortly afterwards my mother was born. Seth had actually been in the country for several years before that, and returned to his native Finland to marry. My father's ancestors, moreover, were a mixture of Norwegian, Danish, German and English, so it is from a combination of these backgrounds that my Nordic looks come.

If I look like Jack Nicklaus, then I consider it a bonus. I will consider it a bigger bonus if I can ever match his record, or get anywhere near it. Nineteen majors. Phew! That is something to aim at.

However, when the Norman family made the move to Brisbane in 1969 I still had three years of schooling ahead of me, and Jack Nicklaus was a name with which I was really not familiar. Perhaps I noticed it while scanning the sports pages, but it hardly registered. That situation would change swiftly and dramatically over the next few years, but in the meantime Aspley High School was demanding my very divided attention.

I had decided in Townsville that my rugby career was finished, and at my new school I turned my football skills to Australian Rules. This is a game based on Gaelic football, and is a far more free-moving code of football than rugby. Melbourne is the Australian stronghold of the game, and when the finals are staged at the famous old Melbourne Cricket Ground crowds in excess of 100,000 are commonplace.

I was selected in a representative Queensland team as a half-forward, and there are probably some of my contemporaries who would say that I was above average at the game. Then, however, I was involved in a football accident that left me with a slightly flattened nose, and eventually changed the course of my life. We had been in Brisbane for only a few months at this stage, and my mother

Air force cadet Norman,
aged fourteen.

had joined Virginia Golf Club just a couple of miles down the road from where we lived.

I was about to be more formally introduced to the game of golf. I am still uncertain of what motivated me to make the offer, but one day when my mother was preparing to leave for her mid-week game I asked, 'Do you mind if I caddie for you?' My main reason for making the offer was to fill in time.

It was as simple as that.

So we went to Virginia together, and I trailed around behind her, pulling the buggy cart and enjoying the walk. I liked watching her play. I knew she was adept at the game, and after several outings with her I decided it was about time I tried too. If Mum can do it, why can't I, was the question I asked myself.

Anybody who knows anything about golf will understand that there is a swift and deflating answer to that question.

When my mother had finished her round I asked if I could borrow her clubs. No practice fairway for me; I wanted to go straight onto the course and give it a solid whack.

So while Mum and her playing partners retired to the clubhouse for their after-match chat and a few drinks I took her clubs and wandered onto the course to start unravelling the mysteries of golf.

A few went straight, a few went over the fence and a few more were badly mis-hit.

But every now and then I managed to make proper contact. I wanted more of those.

In fact, without realizing it, I was hooked.

I offered to caddie at every opportunity I could, and my mother encouraged me. But now there was a real motive. As soon as Mother finished her round I would take her clubs and set out on my own. Often she would be waiting patiently on the clubhouse steps as I came up the last fairway in failing light. She was anxious to get home and prepare the family's evening meal. Sometimes she would come out of the clubhouse, and if I was nowhere to be seen she would go back inside again and have another drink to fill in time.

It was the sort of situation that could not last. The tug-of-war over my mother's set of golf clubs was disrupting the family routine. One day it was agreed that my new whim should be better catered for, and we started scanning the 'for sale' columns of the local newspapers in search of a reasonably priced second-hand set of clubs. Nothing elaborate — just a basic set with a driving club, a few irons and a putter. They would be enough to keep me amused. We answered several advertisements before we finally found a set that would suit me. One of our leads took us into a seamy quarter of Brisbane. We believed we were answering an advertisement placed by a private seller, but found ourselves in an ill-lit, dingy store crammed full of new and secondhand golf-clubs.

I took one look at my parents and declared 'Let's get out of here.' We were convinced that the store was a clearing-house for stolen property, and wanted no part of it.

The next week-end's search was more rewarding, and at 15½ years of age I found myself the owner of my first set of golf-clubs. It was 8 August 1970. They had cost my parents around $150.00.

I joined Virginia Golf Club as a junior member, where my first handicap was the limit of 27.

Now my mother could get home in time to cook the evening meal.

The game consumed me.

My mother would pick me up from school each day sharp at 3.00 p.m. and drive me to Virginia, where I stayed on the practice fairway or played the course until it was impossible to see a ball in flight. We had a prearranged signal. When I had finished playing I would dial our telephone number, let it ring twice, hang up and wait for my lift home.

It saved me ten cents.

I have always been a strong advocate of the practice fairway, and even today I guess I spend more time than most players doing golf's homework. It is the only place to sort out problems and experiment with new ideas, and I have never regretted the hours I put in as a youngster.

It was Virginia professional John Klatt who probably first instilled into me the value of the practice fairway. As the son of members I was eligible to take part in Klatt's regular Saturday morning instructional classes even before I joined the club. He drilled us in every aspect of the game, and it was to those basics I learned from Klatt that I owe my golf game today. My new clubs had plenty of work in the succeeding few months, and my reward was a handicap that started to shrink gradually away from the limit mark.

Although I had been well bitten by the golf bug my other interests were not ignored, and my school chum Greg Lyons and I made ample time to surf. He was also instrumental in getting us both jobs at the Australian Match Manufacturing company, the headquarters of which were not far from Aspley.

Beach fishing off the Queensland coast. I was sixteen years old.

We worked there in school holidays through our early teen years, and it did not take me long to realize that there were easier ways of making a dollar.

Thirty-foot-long logs were trucked into the yard daily, and it was our job to chain-saw them into three-foot-long 'billets'. Once we had cut them into the shorter lengths we grabbed each billet with a hook in either hand and tipped them into a vat of boiling water and left them there for four hours.

It was back-breaking work.

At the end of the boiling period we hooked the billets out of the vat, clasped them between our knees and with a two-handed knife scraped off the soft outer layer of skin and bark before sending them onto the next process.

We worked in jeans and army boots, stripped to the waist. There was quite a knack in clasping those hot logs between our knees and turning them as we scraped off the outer layer. We were paid about $50 a week, and it was money I tucked away in the bank, because already I was dreaming of another set of golf clubs. This time it would be a full set, and I would pay for them myself.

The 25th of April is a significant date for all Australians. It is the day the country commemorates the First World War landing of Australian and New Zealand troops at Gallipoli. On that day in 1971 my father Mervyn and myself teamed up in a four-ball stableford event at Virginia, and I won my first golf trophy. I was on a handicap of 21, and Dad and I shared the winning 50 points we scored almost equally, but the handicapper had no mercy and I was slashed four shots to 17.

By July I was on 11. It was only a matter of a few weeks more before I reached single figures, and the members of Virginia were wondering where it was going to end. I was nominated for a Queensland Golf Union junior squad for which the handicap limit was 6. When the club put my name forward for the state squad they told me they were really breaking the rules, so to justify their action I must play to 6. I was playing comfortably to 9, and if my handicap had been fiddled a little no damage was done and Virginia's little secret was well kept.

They were trying to help me. In those early days the members repeatedly said to my parents, 'It must stop soon. He cannot keep coming down at this rate. He must level out.' It made me more determined, and before I left school in 1972 I was on scratch.

It had taken just over two years.

As juniors we took our golf seriously, and the Queensland Golf Union kept its young state squad busy with well-controlled and organized practice sessions under professional supervision. It was after one of these sessions that one of our team members Steve Perrin almost lost his life. We were all enjoying a few drinks around the swimming-pool of one of our team-mates when Perrin declared that he could swim six lengths of the pool under water. 'I'll show you,' he called with all the bravado of youth, and he dived into the pool. One, two, three lengths of the pool he covered comfortably as we sat and sipped our soft drinks … and then he stopped … on the bottom of the pool.

None of us were really taking much notice of him. We had all tried the same thing before, and it was a regular challenge to see how far we could swim under water. For no reason I glanced down at the pool and realized Steve was not moving.

'God! He's in trouble.'

Fully clothed, I dived into the pool and brought him to the surface. His eyes were dilated and he was hardly breathing. I yelled to Glen Cogill, 'Quick! Get the ambulance! I thought he was only kidding us down there, but he's nearly gone.' While Cogill raced to the telephone I gave Steve mouth-to-mouth resuscitation. For several minutes I worked frantically over his still body. Around us stood the other members of the team, urging and praying that we could breathe life back into our mate. By the time the ambulance arrived Steve Perrin was barely breathing — but he was — and he was whisked away to hospital, where he finally made a full recovery. The time I spent as a life-saver at Magnetic Island had been put to good use.

While my handicap was tumbling in those two years at Virginia I passed several significant landmarks in my brief golfing career.

The most important was my first victory in the 1973 Queensland junior championship at Royal Queensland Golf Club, where two rounds of 73, 74, gave me a five-shot victory over the field. My total of 147 was one under par, and I have had few victories that have satisfied me more.

A reason to smile. I had just won the 1973 Queensland Junior Championship. I still have the hat.

People in the right places in Queensland golf were really starting to notice me, and I was selected earlier that year in the junior Queensland team and went through the series, losing only once to the Victorian Peter Sweeney. It was not a bad loss, as Sweeney is still ranked in the top echelon of Australia's amateur golfers.

Later the same year I was chosen in the senior state side, and went through that series in Perth, Western Australia, without losing a match. I felt I was in good company because the other two players with an unblemished record were both former Australian amateur champions, John Muller and Harry Berwick.

Bob Witcher is an American business-man who moved to sunny Queensland to live several years ago. He is also a close friend of Gary Player, and has been so for many years. Witcher is a golf fanatic, and he established one of Australia's best junior golf tournaments when he asked Player if he would lend his name to a tournament to be known as the Gary Player Junior Classic. The event was over 72 holes and promoted with all the trimmings of a major title, and on the two occasions I competed in the event I won it. Each year's winner was presented with a white blazer plus the appropriate pocket in an unashamed copying of the U.S. Masters.

It was an event which really left its mark in junior golf, and after my victory in the Queensland junior title nothing has given me more satisfaction than to win the Gary Player Junior Classic. The first time I played it was staged at Gailes Golf Club just outside Brisbane and I won by four strokes with a total of 295, making up a four-shot leeway in the last two rounds. My third round of 70 was 3 under par, and a junior record for the course.

In 1973 I won my second club championship at Virginia, and the following year the Norman family moved its golf allegiance across town and we all joined Royal Queensland Golf Club. In 1974 my mother Toini and myself won our club championships at Royal Queensland.

And I started to play for big stakes.

CHAPTER 4
RIDING THE ROLLERS

After I left Aspley High School in 1972 with a shaky pass in my final exams the next couple of years were critical.

I had to start thinking of a career. My father had already come to terms with the fact that I would not follow him into the engineering business, and I was well aware of his disappointment.

It was a way of life that had no appeal to me. I was keen to pursue a Physical Education degree course, but my high-school standard was not good enough for university entry. My father and I went to the Royal Australian Air Force recruiting office in Brisbane and discussed an Air Force career, but I was discouraged by the years of study required.

So in early 1973 my life was aimless.

It was a problem that my parents and I spent many hours discussing, and the more I thought it over the more the idea of a professional golf career appealed to me, though it did not please my parents. I had reached a level in amateur golf where I believed I had a game that could be built to stand the rigours of the professional life if I decided to dedicate myself completely. Without ever resolving my problems I turned to my other great outdoor love — the surf. I guess I used it for many months as a form of escapism, and for most of 1973 I was a 'beach bum'. In Australia's social structure the term is not flattering.

In my final year at Aspley High School I had been a prefect along with my close friend Greg Lyons. As prefects we had privileges, and as prefects we abused those privileges. Often when we knew the surf was running we would walk out of school at lunchtime, go home, pick up our surf-boards and head for Noosa Heads.

Noosa is nearly fifty miles up the coast from Brisbane, and when the waves are breaking it is a board-rider's paradise. It was irresponsible behaviour, but it was a wonderful way to avoid the dreariness of the classroom — and we were never questioned.

Those truant days sparked a love affair between myself and the abundant pleasures that Noosa could offer. When I finally left school my priorities were shared between golf and the surf, and in what order it really does not matter. When I had to play golf I was always there, but in between tournaments I headed for Noosa. Sometimes we had the use of a beachfront flat in which to stay, but mostly we pitched a tent on the foreshore and slept there.

Opposite
Try it sometime. It is not as easy as it looks.

33

Back in the early seventies when I worshipped the sun and the surf.

My hair had grown down to my shoulders.

I shared that existence with two old school-friends of mine, Phillip Martin and Andrew Renshaw — both young men at a loose end like myself — unsure of what the future held for us, and hardly caring. At first light we would be on the beach assessing the value of the waves, and if the surf was 'up' we were in the water straight away.

The freedom and independence of the surfie's existence, the sheer thrill of riding those great rollers into the beach, had a magnetic attraction for me. We came out of the surf when we were hungry and warmed a tin of beans or fried an egg over an open fire. A surfie's needs are simple. Somewhere to sleep, something to eat and our uncomplicated lifestyle made every tomorrow plenty of time to come to grips with the problems of the future.

However, the lack of money and the sheer repetitive sameness of each wave started to bore me. The challenge had disappeared, and I was broke. We were all aware that the Noosa honeymoon could not last for ever, and for me it ended abruptly and in fear.

It was mid-morning, a day or so after a cyclone had swept through the area, that I left our camp alone in search of a wave. There was a heavy swell running

34

in the aftermath of the cyclone, and I decided not to take my board but to rely on flippers and hydrofoil hand controls favoured by body surfers.

To catch a wave I hiked along the headland that pushes out to sea, perhaps 1,000 yards, and then waited for the right one to come along before jumping into it from the rocks.

I selected the wrong wave. Instead of catching a breaker I could comfortably ride into the beach, I found myself on an uncontrollable dumper. In a few seconds I was pushed many feet under and being rolled around along the ocean bed. It was like being inside a washing machine, and I was terrified. The flippers were torn from my feet, and I lost my hand controls in that angry surf.

It took many seconds to struggle back to the surface and a gulp of fresh air. The beach was still nearly half a mile away, and I half drifted, half swam the distance until I eventually felt sand under my feet. When I reached the beach I fell face downwards and stayed there for nearly fifteen minutes ... utterly exhausted.

I was lucky to be alive. I thought I could have died.

I needed very little convincing to turn my back on the surf for ever, and I have not ridden a wave since.

Later that year I accepted a job in the Brisbane warehouse of the Sydney-based company Precision Golf Forgings. It was a stopgap job primarily aimed at filling the big hole in my private economy. My boss was the well-known amateur golfer Sommie Mackay, whose brother the late Ken 'Slasher' Mackay was a regular in Australia's Test cricket teams for many years.

When I took the job it was on the understanding that I would work from 7.00 a.m. to 11.00 a.m. and then have the rest of the day off for practice at Virginia. To get to Virginia I had my eyes set on a train that left Brisbane's Roma Street station punctually at 11.20 a.m., and if I missed it there was nearly an hour to wait for the next one. PGF's warehouse was on the other side of Brisbane, about a mile from the railway station.

I worked hard and conscientiously for my new masters, arriving punctually every morning and making up parcels for dispatch at a furious rate. It was a menial task. I packed and boxed golf-clubs, golf-bags, buggies and the whole range of equipment merchandized by PGF, and I packed them fast. In the four-hour shift to which I was committed every day I got away sometimes fifty separate parcels, and I was proud that I made up more than anybody else in the place.

Mackay was a tough boss. I kept my eye on the clock in the best trade-union tradition, but so often he found one extra parcel to make up as the clock hands ticked towards eleven. I would be furious. If I missed that 11.20 train then I also missed an hour of practice. Whenever Sommie found an extra chore for me I would throw him an angry look, put the parcel together in double-quick time and run out of the place.

The few minutes it took to pack and dispatch that extra load meant a sprint to the railway station. Many times I weaved and dodged my way through the pedestrian traffic in Brisbane's main streets as I raced for the train. I did not miss it once, but there were many close calls. Often the guard would be blowing his whistle and waving the train out of the platform as I fell into a carriage. In the twenty-minute ride to Virginia station I would get my breath back and be ready for my daily five-hour session on the practice fairway.

One of the factors that made my job at PGF more tolerable was that a close friend of mine from Virginia Golf Club, Roger Dwyer, was also employed by the company. Better than anybody else, he understood why I turned to the surf as an escape route for the problems I was trying to sort out in my mind. He was a confidant I valued, and it was with him that I would discuss my hopes and ambitions one day to turn professional. The link between us is still firm. He was older than me, and a good listener.

In 1973 the Australian Open was set down for Royal Queensland, and I lodged an entry.

Roger Dwyer offered to caddie for me. It was my first Australian Open championship, and I was looking forward to matching my fledgling skills against the cream of Australia's amateurs and professionals and the overseas players imported for the tournament. My local record was impressive, and here was a chance to trade shots with the best players in the land. Privately I believed the experience of playing a tournament of the stature of an Australian Open would also be a great yardstick for my professional ambitions. With Dwyer as my caddie I was well pleased with the first three rounds of the tournament, shooting 71, 76, 71, a score which saw me sharing the position of leading amateur alongside the Western Australian Terry Gale, now a prominent player on the professional circuit. We were only a few shots away from the leaders, and I went into the final round firmly believing that I had a chance not only to beat Terry Gale but even to win the title.

So much for dreams.

On the final day Gale and I were drawn alongside each other, and the fight for top amateur became a personal battle between us. The 10th hole at Royal Queensland is an innocent par 4, and by the time we reached it any belief that I could shoot a miracle round and get among the leaders had gone. Gale had chipped in twice for birdies early in the final round, and I was trailing him by a couple of shots at the halfway mark.

Winning the amateur section very quickly became my top priority. My second shot found a greenside bunker at the 10th, and while Roger Dwyer moved to the back of the green and parked my buggy at the bottom of the slope I settled my feet into the sand. I knew I had to play a good shot and hold par to stop Gale getting further ahead of me. Nevertheless, I was to watch in despair as my ball trickled across the green, past the flag and then start to roll down the hill.

Roger had left the clubs unattended while he moved a few yards away to talk to friends.

Disaster! My ball hit my buggy. It was a two-shot penalty.

I was seething with anger as I chipped the ball back up the slope and finally holed out for an 8 that wiped me from contention. As we left the next tee I turned furiously on Roger and demanded to know why he had been careless enough to leave my buggy where he had. 'Do you know what you have cost me?' I said angrily.

Poor Roger. He put an arm over my shoulder and said, 'One day you are going to be a great player. Rome was not built in a day and you will have many more bad breaks. I'm sorry.'

For the first and only time on a golf-course I burst into tears. I grabbed my towel from my golf-bag and draped it over my head to hide my misery.

I took a double-bogey at the 11th.

I have often wondered since if Terry Gale was aware of my tears. If he was then he has never mentioned it to me in the years we have been playing together as professionals.

My game came together again as the round drew to a close and an eagle and a couple of birdies in the final holes left me with a closing 77. My total of 295 was five shots behind Terry, who finished with an excellent 72 for a total of 290 and leading amateur spot.

The tournament was won by the American J. C. Snead, a nephew of the great Sam Snead, but I did not stay around for the presentation ceremony. I had finished second amateur, and should have been there to receive my trophy. When I was called for and did not answer it was a misdemeanour that did not endear me to the governing body of Australian golf.

The same situation was to occur again later in my career.

But at Royal Queensland in 1973 I just wanted to get away.

CHAPTER 5
SYDNEY — AND BACK

Packing parcels at PGF, racing for trains that I almost missed and playing tournaments was the way 1974 drifted by as my plans to quit amateur golf started to firm in my mind. There were many successful moments which fuelled my ambition to turn golf into a career, but making the step was to prove more complex than I realized. During the year I won the Royal Queensland Club title, and when my mother was also successful in the associates championship, the Norman family had set a club record that is unlikely to be beaten.

My mother and father had reconciled themselves by now that I would turn professional, and I was very conscious that neither of them were overjoyed about it. I am certain that both my parents would have been happier to see me settle into a solid office-type job and continue my golf as an amateur.

I started to make inquiries about the switch. I knew when I made it the timing had to be perfect, and as far as I was concerned it had to remain a tight secret until all the loose ends were tied together. But I was appalled at the situation I discovered existed in Queensland.

To me, turning professional meant only one thing — playing tournaments for a living as soon as I could — yet I understood that there was a training and probationary period that every young professional must serve. He must learn to service members properly, make clubs and keep them polished. He had to pick up balls from the practice fairway after his master had given lessons. I could not believe that the training period would last three years. I was nearing my twentieth birthday, and three years sounded like a life sentence. But they were the rules of the Queensland PGA, and it was by those rules that I must abide. Or must I?

I used the resources of PGF to make further inquiries in New South Wales, and finally one of Australia's most famous golf mentors, Billy McWilliam, agreed to employ me as a trainee.

McWilliam had caused a sensation as a player when he holed a full 6-iron shot on the last hole at Royal Queensland to lead the second post-war Australian Open golf title in 1947. His final-hole eagle gave him a course record of 65, and it was not until the final round of that championship that the ultimate winner, the late Ossie Pickworth, finally caught him.

But McWilliam made his name more as a shrewd talent-spotter than as a player. It was he who first discovered and developed the remarkable talents of

Bruce Crampton and Bruce Devlin, both previous winners of the Australian Open and both now living in America. Crampton was the first Australian to win a million dollars on the American tour, and was one of the first ten players to achieve that figure.

I was delighted that my first steps in professional golf were to be guided by such a man. McWilliam had been given an assurance by the NSW section of the PGA that I would be released to play tournaments by invitation from his shop during my trainee time, and that undertaking was better than any I could get in my native Queensland.

I chose to keep my move into professional golf a secret as long as I could, and local newspapers published an article saying that I had been transferred by Precision Golf Forgings to their Sydney headquarters. The truth was that I had an obligation to play in an amateur event and did not want to break it, despite having already made the decision to go professional.

On 5 March 1975, just a few weeks after my twentieth birthday, the story broke that I had turned professional and was leaving Brisbane for a trainee professional's job with McWilliam.

When I set off for Sydney on the biggest gamble of my life I had the full support of my parents. I appreciated it. My future had caused many moments of trauma, but now a decision had been reached. I owned a small car of my own (bought with the money I had earned from PGF), and it was agreed that I should drive to Sydney. Both my parents helped pack my worldly belongings into the back of my little Cortina. I kissed Mother goodbye and shook hands with my father as I drove away from our two-storey home in Aspley on a journey from which there was no turning back — at least, not for several hours.

I must have been three hours down the main highway towards Sydney when a thought flashed across my mind. 'Where is my money?' I pulled the car into the side of the road and started a search of my pockets and luggage that proved fruitless. I had planned to bring my life-savings of $2,000 to Sydney with me, but had obviously forgotten to pick the money up before I drove away from home.

Three hours later I was back home, and my mother greeted me with 'You obviously heard the broadcast.' 'What broadcast? I did not hear any broadcast,' I told her.

My mother then explained that shortly after I had driven out she had discovered the cash in the house and had immediately telephoned the local radio station, to which she knew I would be tuned on the long drive south. The message she asked the radio station to broadcast was 'Would Greg Norman, heading south to Sydney, please return home. He has forgotten his money.'

My mother said she reinforced the radio call with 'thought messages' to me and still claims they made me stop. I certainly did not consciously hear the radio call. Perhaps subconsciously I had heard it, or perhaps my mother's 'thought messages' had worked. One thing was certain. I was finding strange obstacles on my path to a professional golf career.

I was a long way behind schedule when I finally reported to Billy McWilliam at Beverley Park Golf Club.

Life at Beverley Park was rigorous but fair. I shared the pro-shop chores with another trainee, Doug Murray, and it was with him that I also shared an apartment in suburban Kogarah, close to the golf-course.

I set myself a practice timetable that had me out of bed at 4 o'clock every

Opposite
Searching for the horizon.
It has come closer since
this mid-seventies
Brisbane picture.

40

morning. By 5 o'clock, when it was just light enough to see, I started hitting balls, and would keep at it until I was due to open the doors of the pro shop at 7.30. These were the only hours that I could find during the day to work on my game. Once the doors were open for business I was in the shop repairing clubs or looking after customers until my day's work finished at 5 p.m.

But then I started work at night. McWilliam also conducted a night driving range, and Murray and myself worked on alternate nights selling buckets of balls to the customers. When the lights were finally turned off around 10.50 p.m. and the players drifted away to their beds our job was to retrieve the balls from the fairway and get them sorted out for the next night. Most nights there were 3,000 or 4,000 balls to pick up. It was a hard grind. Usually when I got back to our apartment later at night Doug would be still awake, and as we drifted off to sleep we 'bitched' about the life. We agreed that we were spending too much time in the shop and on the driving range and not getting enough time to practise and play. 'I am going nowhere fast,' I told myself.

The whole object of coming to Sydney to serve my time as a trainee was to cut short the period I would be confined to life in the pro shop. I had come south on the understanding that the New South Wales PGA would release me for tournaments during the year, but at the end of May I learned there had been a change of mind and I was to be held to the full three years as a trainee ... and no tournament golf! I felt betrayed and angry.

I rang my parents in Brisbane and told them the news. 'I am stuck here. They have just told me I can't get out for three years.'

McWilliam also reacted angrily to the decision of the NSW trainee department, and his criticism was published. 'Greg Norman is one of the most talented assistants I have ever had but he is going back home because he cannot play in pro tournaments in Sydney. He has been waiting for invitations to play that have never arrived so now he is going back to Queensland.'

Although I had found plenty to complain about during my few months at Beverley Park, it was nice to know that McWilliam rated me so highly. It was not his fault that I had been denied the chance to play tournaments, nor was it his fault that the people in charge of trainees in New South Wales had backed away from their undertaking.

Remember, I was still the reigning club champion at Royal Queensland, and it was to the head professional of that club, Charles Earp, that I turned for help. I spelled out my position to Earp in a long and costly telephone call, but it was all worth it when he said, 'Come on back. I will put you on.' He already had two trainees under his control, and by putting me on the staff too he was (as I well knew) stretching himself further than he should.

Three months after I had headed south to Sydney to start my professional life I was heading back to Brisbane.

Greg Norman had every reason to feel frustrated.

I thanked McWilliam for his help, and said goodbye to Doug Murray, hoping he would find another co-tenant for our apartment. We had formed a firm friendship. Murray was a wonderful player, but I rarely saw him after my Sydney experience, and I believe he drifted away from the game.

I decided to make the 500-mile drive back to Brisbane at night, and set out at 10.00 p.m. on a clear winter's night, expecting to arrive back home at Aspley early next morning. I had plenty to ponder over as my little Cortina sped through the night towards home. Working back in the pro shop of the club where I was reigning champion would be an experience. How would the members take it? My parents were both members at Royal Queensland — what would their feelings be? Would Charlie Earp finally be able to help me actually *play* as a professional?

It was around 4.00 a.m. when I glimpsed the big grey kangaroo leap out of the tree-line beside the road. It bounded in from my left. Instinctively I swung the wheel hard left to avoid it — and then the crash came. My car slammed into a direction post on the side of the road, spun twice and came to rest on the opposite side of the road with its back jammed into an embankment.

For several minutes I sat in the car, shaken and dazed. I had missed the kangaroo — but at a price. In the darkness I slowly unfastened my seat-belt, eased myself out of the driver's seat and summed up the damage as best I could. I convinced myself the car was drivable, and that belief was confirmed when I switched on the ignition and the motor ticked over. I nursed the car off the embankment and back onto the road, and at daybreak pulled up in the driveway at Aspley.

It was a badly shaken young man who headed straight for his bedroom, and for the next seven hours I slept soundly.

When I awoke early in the afternoon I went down to have a closer look at the damage. I broke down. The car was an absolute write-off. The left side and rear were wrecked, and how I drove it the last hundred miles or so I will never understand. But the damage was even more deep-seated: the impact of the crash had split the fuel tank, and on the concrete driveway an ominous pool of petrol had formed. It was still dripping as I watched. Just one spark ...

For the second time I felt lucky to be alive. The car had cost me $2,300 and was not insured. The repairs cost me $1,200, and when they were completed I sold it.

When my stop-start life as a professional golfer resumed with Charlie Earp I was struggling financially, but I felt no sense of defeatism returning to Brisbane.

I was back in familiar surroundings this time, with an assurance that the Queensland PGA would issue invitations for me to compete in events under its control. Of course Charlie Earp had to agree, and when he told the Press 'Greg will be released if he does his homework' I made certain I did just that.

CHAPTER 6
LEARNING THE PRO GAME

When I started work in the shop at Royal Queensland in the middle of 1975 my salary was $38 a week. Because I had bought another car to replace my now discarded Cortina with the proceeds of its sale, plus the rest of my life-savings, the few dollars a week I was earning were stretched to the limit. My parents understood the situation I was in, and I lived at home without paying a cent in board and lodging, but I was expected to run my own car and keep myself in clothes.

My budgeting was carefully planned. They were stringent times.

The conditions of my employment with 'the boss' gave me ample time for practice, as every other day I was given the afternoon off on the proviso that I spent it on the fairway. Whenever time permitted Earp would wander down to the practice mound and watch me hit shots, finding a fault here and there, but always encouraging me. He could see I was a willing worker.

I tackled my pro-shop chores with more enthusiasm than I had during those few months in Sydney, because now I was working towards an attainable goal.

The Queensland trainee championship was only a couple of months away, and I would be able to test myself under tournament conditions once again. It had been a long time since my last competitive round of golf.

Before trainee professionals, under the Australian PGA's system, are thrown into the maelstrom of tournament golf they are given a thorough grounding in all facets of the game. For those trainees who see professional golf as a teaching and merchandise-retailing career the syllabus devised by the PGA is an invaluable foundation. It does not matter what the trainee's ambitions are, he must pass the business management course and the other subjects set down by the PGA before he can become a fully fledged professional. It is the choice of the individual as to whether he makes the tournament circuit his career or seeks the life of a club professional.

Whatever his choice, the basic training is still the same. Apart from my work in the shop and on the practice fairway, I devoted many hours to the bookwork demands of my chosen career, and in the first six months of my time at Royal Queensland I sat and passed all the examinations normally reserved for the completion of the three-year trainee term.

I was well pleased with the results. I topped the state.

In September 1975 I teed up in the Queensland trainee championship, and

after four rounds tied with Gerry Taylor on 291 before winning the championship in a play-off.

It was a quaint tournament. The first two rounds were played at Keperra Golf Club, and at the halfway mark I had fired 67-74 and trailed Taylor by two shots after he had returned 68-71. We played on a Monday. The championship had to fit into our pro-shop duties, and because all trainees were given Mondays off, that was the only day of the week we could play. On the Monday after the first two rounds our bosses cancelled our day off and all the trainees were instructed to caretake the shops while the senior professionals competed in a pro-am event.

So there were many edgy young professionals around Brisbane for the next fortnight as the long count-down to the final 36 holes ticked by.

The venue for the last two rounds was the McLeod Country Club, one of the most unique golf-clubs in Australia. It was built for women by women, and it is the men whose membership is closely screened before they are admitted as 'associates'.

I drew level with Taylor when I returned a 71 in the third round to his 73, and we both missed many opportunities in the final round, with each of us taking 79. Almost three weeks after the tournament started I finally won the 18-hole play-off, and I was an excited young man as I drove home that night with the good news. It was a victory that rated a small mention in the Brisbane press, but to the Norman family and to Charlie Earp it had special significance.

When I defended the title the following year I won by 15 shots, but by then the Australian PGA had issued me the priceless invitation I had been striving for.

My first ambition was to be a pilot and the Royal Air Force gave me a taste of the life in October 1981. Flight Lieutenant John Mardon at the controls — and I can't three-putt from here!

For three months I was to be allowed to play the major tournaments on the Australian circuit.

Charlie Earp ran a tight ship in his pro shop, and for the practice privileges he allowed me I had to work hard. Like most youngsters of my age, I was perhaps a little selfish, perhaps expecting too much latitude, and I quickly discovered that Earp was not a man to cross. If Charlie believed any of his assistants were not working hard enough his dismissal routine was simple and unmistakable.

'There's the door. What's your hurry?' and more than one youngster's golf ambitions came to an end with those words.

Sometimes he would help them out the door by the scruff of the neck.

It was around lunchtime this day that our tempers became frayed. I believed I had contributed a good morning's work and was due for a stretch on the practice fairway when he ordered me into the back of the shop to clean several sets of clubs.

I rebelled.

For a moment I believed I was going to get the scruff-of-the-neck treatment. He ordered me out of the shop but I stood my ground, and as our tempers cooled I did as I was told and set to work cleaning clubs.

It was the only clash we had in an otherwise harmonious relationship, and I blame myself for it. It would be difficult to estimate what I owe that man in terms of encouragement, friendship and understanding.

A few minutes after the temperature dropped my mother walked into the shop and I sold her a golf-ball and a packet of tees. She was never aware of the flare-up.

Later in my golf career Norman Von Nida, David Graham and Jack Nicklaus were all to help streamline my golf game, but its solid basis I owe to Charlie Earp.

Everybody who plays golf has enjoyed the fun of a small wager on the outcome of his Saturday afternoon four-ball event. Betting is an accepted way of life at every golf club I know, whether it is for a new ball or a few dollars on the out, home and match. It adds spice to the game, and I have known captains of industry battle their hearts out for a few dollars. They handle their golf-course wagers as seriously as their company balance-sheets.

From the time I started playing at Virginia I started to bet. It was hard to avoid. The stakes were never large, and winning and losing did not hurt either side, apart from a small dent in one's pride. However, now that I was in the shop at Royal Queensland betting assumed vastly different proportions, and I became involved. I played regularly with the same group of members, and our matches were always played on Wednesday and Sunday afternoons. On the salary I was being paid I couldn't afford to lose, and the chance to supplement my income was a spur for my efforts on the practice fairway. I used to look forward eagerly to those two afternoons of the week.

I clearly remember the first time I stood on the first tee and the stakes were settled at $20 a side and $40 for the match. I gulped. If I lost I knew I had just enough money to cover the bet. But if I won then I had more than doubled my week's salary.

When my partner and I walked off the final green not only had we won both nines but had taken the match too.

When I arrived home that night I presented my mother with the best-quality box of chocolates I could buy. 'Here is a present for you,' I said.

I was at Royal Queensland for nearly eighteen months, and during that period my parents were never aware of the extent of my golf-course gambling.

They would have been horrified.

As the months wore on the stakes grew higher and my financial situation improved. I spent every spare minute on the practice fairway. I was learning how to play for money. Of course, there were losing days, but they were far outweighed by the number of times I was on the winning side. I kept my gambling proceeds apart from my normal income, and was never embarrassed by not being able to cover a losing bet. Every golfer who has played for side-bets knows the snowballing effect it can have, particularly on the loser, who is always anxious to double-up next time to try and get his money back.

The biggest win I had was $1,200, and it came close to the end of my time with Charlie Earp, as I was preparing to play the Australian circuit.

It was that money that helped finance me on the tour.

I will not mention the names of the other three players in the group, but when we left the first tee the stakes were $100 for each nine holes, and $200 for the winner of the match with the usual options. With four holes to play, my partner and I had won everything — both nines and the match. Our opponents had strokes at three of the next four holes, and as any red-blooded gambler would do, elected to press for $300. By the time we reached the 18th tee we had overcome them again, and were now winning a handsome $700 with just one hole left to play. I still owed one of our opponents a stroke at the 18th, and when they exercised their right to a further option of $500 my partner and I readily agreed to let them on. If we lost the hole we would still win $200, and if we won it then our afternoon's golf would be worth $1,200 each.

The last hole at Royal Queensland is a par 4, and that day I reached it with a sand-iron pitch for my second shot after pummelling a big drive down the fairway. My second shot finished about 12 feet from the hole, pin-high, and when I rolled it home for a birdie it settled the issue and made me a whole lot richer.

There was always tremendous tension in our four-ball encounters, but no matter how fierce the rivalry on the golf-course it was all forgotten as we enjoyed our after-match drinks and went through the ritualistic post-mortems. When the banter and celebrating finished the winners treated the losers to dinner. Then we would all go back to the house of one of our group and play snooker into the small hours.

They were days I remember fondly — when close and lasting friendships were forged. If Joss Butterfield, John Bell, Tyrell Stafford, David Livingstone, Charlie King and Cyril King ever happen to read this book I want them to know how much I enjoyed those days together. They were an important part of my formative years, and the friendship between Cyril King and myself has become an even stronger bond since.

The anonymity that had virtually hidden me since I joined Charlie Earp in mid-1975 was about to be removed. In April 1976 the Queensland PGA announced that I was now eligible to compete as an invitee in state-controlled tournaments, and more importantly, to accept any prize money I might win. The invitation was backed by the chairman of the trainee committee, professional Peter Barry, who said, 'Greg has done exceptionally well in his exams and so it was no trouble recommending him for an invitation to play.' Behind the invitation was undoubtedly the influence of Charlie Earp.

The move by the Queensland PGA still restricted me to events played under its jurisdiction, but it was the first toehold towards the broader Australian scene and its tournament riches.

I played my first pro-am event at Dalby early in June, and finished high in the order but without ever threatening to win.

I played in every tournament for which I was eligible, winning several minor pro-am events and building up my bank balance and my confidence.

Early in August 1976 the letter for which I had been waiting arrived. The National PGA invited me to join the lucrative Australian tour due to start in just a few weeks, and I was ecstatic. A few days later at Keperra I shot rounds of 76, 68, 72, 72 to retain my state trainee title by a whopping 15 shots. Could it be only fifteen months ago that I had left Sydney in despair, wondering if I was ever going to set foot on the professional tour? The Australian PGA had shown it had faith in my ability, and I resolved that I would show that this was well placed. And the only place to do that was on the golf-course.

The first tournament I played in was a $15,000 event in Bateman's Bay, where I finished third. It was a good start. The following week the first major title on the circuit for 1976 was our own Queensland Open, set down for Keperra and carrying prize money of $18,000. It was small by national standards, but the size of the purse was immaterial to me as I prepared to play an important title in front of my home-town friends for the first time. The field was much stronger than at Bateman's Bay, with players like Stewart Ginn, Ted Ball, Guy Wolstenholme, Roger Davis and the Americans Jim Ahern, Mike Reid and Art Russell all seeking the $3,000 first prize.

My four rounds were 70, 73, 74, 70 for a total of 287 and a share of third place with former Australian PGA champion Mike Cahill, Victorian Peter Croker and the talented American Mike Reid.

The tournament was won by my fellow-Queenslander John Dyer, who survived several crises in the final round to win by three shots from the American Ahern. Dyer was the first Queenslander in ten years to take out the championship, and his winning score of 282 was only five shots ahead of mine.

I had every reason to feel pleased with my first two weeks on the tour, and when I studied the scores of the players who finished behind me in the Queensland Open I felt confident of an early break-through.

The *Brisbane Courier Mail* had this to say about my performance : 'Throughout the tournament he missed only ten greens. He laid into his tee shot off the 18th for a gain of 360 metres and hit a 9 iron in. For a 21 year old not yet out of his time it was downright arrogance.'

A top ten finish in the New South Wales Open followed, and then it was off to Adelaide for the $35,000 West Lakes Classic — the first of the 'big money' titles on the Australian circuit. I invited my close friend Glen Cogill to come too and caddie for me. We had been members of both Queensland's junior and senior amateur teams together, and he understood my game intimately. He accepted the invitation.

I was pleased, because it turned out to be an exciting week for both of us.

CHAPTER 7
'THE TOUGHEST PLACE...'

If Utopia could be measured by human definitions then I believe I found it in Adelaide during four days of October 1976. Fate preordained that period of magic at The Grange Golf Club where the blond kid from Queensland overnight found himself a celebrity.

The success that came to me in Australia's beautiful cathedral city was undoubtedly the first stepping-stone along the road to the position I now enjoy in world golf. I am not certain just what that position is, but of one thing I am aware — it is a great deal more secure than it was when I flew into Adelaide to tee up in the $35,000 West Lakes Classic, the first of the major titles on the spring circuit of 1976.

I had won an award in Queensland offered by an Australian golf-shoe manufacturer, and it was as a guest of that company that I made the trip south. Certainly I would have played in the tournament anyway, but the air fare and hotel expenses that went with the prize enabled me to bring Glen Cogill along with me. As my close friend and caddie, he walked the upper air of those four days alongside me, and relished them as much as I did.

My few tournament performances in the north of the country had completely escaped the more influential golf-writers in Australia's south, and except for one or two I was just another hopeful kid teeing up in his first real major.

All the greats of Australian golf came to Adelaide that year to wrestle for the prize money, and the pre-tournament discussion hinged around the impending clash between that pair of globetrotters David Graham and Graham Marsh. David Graham had won the World Match Play championship, the American Golf Classic and the Chunichi Crowns Invitational tournament in Japan during the year, and although jaded from his travels was expected to win in Adelaide, while Marsh had also enjoyed a highly successful year on the foreign circuit.

Both players came to Adelaide riding form streaks that singled them out ahead of the rest. And the 'rest' included Bruce Crampton, Bruce Devlin, Billy Dunk, Bob Shearer and Jack Newton, as well as many other talented Australian and overseas players.

The Grange was a course of contrasts, with many holes wide open and receptive to my game, but there were many tight, tree-lined holes where I knew I would have to take care.

'It is a tough-looking field,' I said to Cogill. 'I hope I can shoot low enough to

Early in my professional career I had the pleasure of playing a round with President Marcos of the Philippines. We played a round at the Nichols Golf Club in Manila and the President, a keen student of the game, was heavily guarded all the way.

make my expenses.' My draw for the first two days put me alongside the incomparable Bruce Crampton, whose American deeds I had been reading about for years. He reminded me of a Grenadier Guardsman without his busby — tall and straight-backed, and with an air of almost disdainful superiority. Undoubtedly it was a promotional coup to get him to the first tee in Adelaide but appearance money can be a big persuader. We were introduced on the first tee, and shook hands. We exchanged good wishes for the round ahead.

How well I remember that first round.

We were drawn late in the field, which meant occupying myself for several hours before we were called to the tee. I loosened up on the practice fairway for maybe an hour, and then went to the putting green to give that department of my game its final polish. I was like a greyhound on a leash, anxious to get to grips with the course. The delay was irking me. A few minutes before we were called to the tee the news spread that Perth player John Clifford had set a new course record of 67. 'Hell. That's a pretty good score. I'll have to go out and beat it,' I said to myself.

And I did — by a whopping three shots. My first round of 64 catapulted me

50

into the national headlines for the first time in my career, but I went back to my motel that night very conscious that there was a lot more work to do.

The round is worth recalling in some detail. I went out in 31, narrowly missing a hole in one at the short 5th, and at the halfway mark stood a handsome 5 under par.

I had played aggressive golf and played it successfully, and was determined not to retreat into a defence of the position I had secured.

Because the first tee had been running nearly forty minutes late when we set out, dusk was gathering as we worked our way through the final few holes. Crampton's reputation had attracted a fair-sized gallery behind us, but the crowd had swollen to several thousand as we came towards the end of the round. With all modesty, I believe the increased numbers were there to see if I could hang on.

If adrenalin is a factor in sporting success then I probably had more than my fair share as I birdied the 13th, 14th and 15th to go 8 under par and find myself in another world.

Any golfer who has been there will understand what I mean.

The only shot I dropped to par for the day was at the 16th, where my drive caught a bare lie and my second shot came up short of the green. I parred the last two holes to complete a very satisfactory day's work.

The momentum I had generated on the first day of the tournament was there again on the morrow as I slipped around The Grange in 67 and found myself 11 under par and five shots clear of the field.

In the 36 holes played there were 15 birdies to my credit.

As one Sydney critic wrote, 'Flourishing his driver like a sabre Norman again cut a swathe through The Grange club's relatively dull East course. Norman belted two shots to the heart of the green at the 563 yards 15th. It was, said the locals, the first time the green had been reached in two and into a slight breeze to boot.' But the round was not without incident, and it was possibly the intervention of an alert official that saved me from disqualification.

At the short 8th hole my tee shot finished on the surface of a path from which I was entitled to drop. I picked up my ball and indicated to Crampton my quite legal intentions.

I had selected a spot where I could drop but had committed, in Crampton's eyes, the cardinal sin of not marking the spot where my ball had laid originally. He started to give me hell. He is a tough guy at the best of times. I hardly knew him, and he advanced towards me, demanding to know where my marker was. I pointed out the exact spot where the ball had been, while Crampton remonstrated with me. Fortunately, an official stepped forward and supported my case and Crampton seemed quite satisfied.

'How would I know whether or not you are dropping nearer the hole unless there is a marker down?' snapped Crampton.

It taught me a lesson, and whenever I feel I am entitled to a drop these days I always make certain that I mark the original position of the ball.

But there was more to come. After pitching the ball to about six feet I prepared to putt for my par. I was brushing several grains of sand off my line with my hand when Crampton's voice penetrated my concentration.

'You are not allowed to do that,' he said.

'I am,' I replied.

And with more emphasis Crampton repeated his earlier statement: 'You are not allowed to do that.'

An impasse had developed, and was broken only by the same tournament official who had stood by me a few minutes earlier.

It transpired that the current rules of the American PGA tour interpreted the situation differently and my action had been perfectly correct.

I was relieved to put the hole behind me. I had been wrong in one instance and correct in the other, but the combination of the two was unnerving.

Twice in that second round I incurred penalty shots, but overcame them with good recovery shots and putting. Without those penalties my lead would have been even greater at the halfway mark.

I was relieved when I did not draw to play alongside Crampton again, but I must add that he did congratulate me after the first two days. 'You played some great golf,' he said.

After my opening round that doyen of Australian golf, five times British Open champion Peter Thomson, wrote in the *Melbourne Age* :

> All talk then centered on the question of whether his 64 had virtually won him his first golf title. I have my doubts. He showed distinct signs of nervousness as his score reached the sub-normal region of eight under with three holes to play — and he bogeyed the 16th. A five stroke lead over the two internationals is hardly worth counting at this stage. Even so, Norman is without doubt the best looking young golfer I have seen in Australia.

When I read the article I was flattered at the comparisons, but also keen to show Thomson that my opening score would indeed be the cornerstone to my first tour win.

After shooting 66 in the third round I was ten shots in front and 16 under par. My birdie count for the 54 holes played was 22, better than one every three holes.

I started that round with a bogey, and the strong feeling that the rest of the field was waiting for me to come back and join them.

Birdies at the second and third holes stopped the slide, and I felt more in control of my game and my emotions than in the previous two days.

Only an earthquake could stop me from winning now, but no golf tournament of this type is ever won until the last putt is home, and when Cogill and I talked over our tactics for the final day we resolved that we must continue to attack. I do not believe I know how to play otherwise. With one round to play, my closest pursuers were Bruce Crampton and Chris Tickner, both at 6 under par, and they were entitled to believe their score hardly warranted being ten shots away from the lead. Bob Shearer was in a group another shot farther away, while Graham Marsh and Bruce Devlin were twelve shots behind me.

When I fell asleep that night a statement Gary Player once made was firmly in my mind. 'The toughest, loneliest place in the world is out in front of a golf tournament.'

I was to find out how true that was the next day. My determination to keep attacking was all very well in theory, but this time my aggression led me into more trouble than I had found on the other three days of the tournament. I had six bogeys and a double bogey, but fortunately balanced them out with another five birdies.

News travels at a remarkable speed around a golf-course, and as my bogeys started to mount I was well aware that David Graham was charging. At one stage he got to within four shots of me, but I survived the crisis, and came to the final hole needing a par for 73. Behind the green I could see my fellow Queensland professional Bryan Smith standing there with a huge smile on his face and brandishing a bottle of champagne.

When I reached the green Smith called to me, 'Have a drink. You can take six putts from there and still win.'

But I waved him away. The celebrations could come later. I took three putts and finished with a 74, and five shots ahead of David Graham and Graham Marsh, who also came with a late rush to share second place.

I signed my card and accepted Smith's offer. I felt I had earned that swig of champagne.

The first prize of $7,000 was more money than I had ever seen. Along with the $2,000 odd I had won in the few weeks before I came to Adelaide I now found myself close to the top of the Australian Order of Merit, and this was to cause a few headaches for the Australian PGA.

As I said earlier, if this was Utopia then I was there. My victory celebrations were quite restrained, but there were many of my friends who celebrated heartily on my behalf. Even today I find victory very little reason to whoop it up because I go into every tournament with the object of winning. If I am successful, then I have achieved what I set out to do. The players who indulge in elaborate winning celebrations are really the players who don't expect to win, but find that somehow they have.

I believe my attitude is a professional one. I can never understand why America's Jerry Pate finds a lake to jump into every time he has a win. Perhaps it is because those wins are not very frequent.

My win in Adelaide also added another dimension to my education — I learned how to handle myself at a Press Conference. I was the freshest copy Australia's golf-writers had come across for many years, and they squeezed every drop they could from my background. They all stressed the point that I had been playing for only six years, and had taken up the game because my mother Toini played it. My likeness to Jack Nicklaus hardly goes beyond the colour of our hair, but that was enough for the Press to manufacture spin-offs from his Golden Bear tag. I was called the Golden Cub, the Golden Bear Cub and several other variations that did not impress me. I was plain Greg Norman, and preferred it that way.

But unashamedly I admit that Nicklaus was, and still is, my golf idol. I will quote Peter Thomson again. After my West Lakes win he wrote :

> His rounds of 64, 67, 66, 74 speak for themselves but the manner of him getting them revealed that here we have a young golfer in the Nicklaus mould — dare I say better? What incredible heights must now be before him. As each generation builds on the previous and seems to earn more, what an income this man will earn by the time he reaches 30 …

And he went on :

> Nicklaus is something of an idol as he is to every blond teenager with an

My first meeting with the 'Golden Bear', Jack Nicklaus, was at The Australian Golf Club, Sydney. I played with him next day in the first round of the 1976 Australian Open.

interest in golf, but the likeness is remarkable. He not only looks like Nicklaus, he goes through the same preparatory motions.

The following week in Sydney I met Nicklaus for the first time when the Australian Golf Union drew us together for the first two days of the Australian Open. He still jokingly reminds me of how I topped my first tee shot in the opening round.

The Australian spring tour was completed with two tournaments in Melbourne, and I managed an 8th place finish in the Colgate Champion of Champions at Victoria Golf Club, but then missed the cut in the final event of the year at Royal Melbourne.

Tom Watson played in the Colgate tournament, and although he closed with a 66 I finished a shot ahead of him.

Before the Royal Melbourne tournament started I was holding down second position in the Australian Order of Merit, and if I could manage to hold that place then I was in line for World Cup selection. The tournament director of the Australian PGA, Mr Jim Moran, had foreseen the precedent I could set, and he and his committee had studied the rules closely to see if there was any impediment to an invited trainee representing the country. There were several days of deliberation before Moran told me I was eligible — if I qualified.

The PGA had changed the rules to cater for the situation.

While Bob Shearer and Stewart Ginn were battling it out in overtime for the Chrysler Classic at Royal Melbourne I was sitting nervously in the living-room of a friend's house just a few hundred yards from the course.

If Ginn won then he would tip me out of second place in the Order of Merit and join Shearer in the World Cup team.

Shearer was already an automatic selection. For me the tension was almost unbearable.

It was about 5.30 on Sunday afternoon when the telephone rang. 'Shearer has won the tournament and you are in the World Cup team with him,' I was told. I sank back in my chair and cast my mind back over the incredible three months behind me. I was the first trainee professional ever chosen to represent the country. My first few months as a professional golfer had rewarded me beyond anything I had dared hope for.

I pinched myself.

CHAPTER 8
THE MARSHALL PLAN

There were only a few short days between the end of the Australian tournament season and my departure for California with Bob Shearer. The activity in the Norman household at Aspley was feverish. Australia's brand-new World Cup player was on the threshold of his international career, but I thought only of each crowded hour as I prepared for the trip ahead. I had never owned a passport before — because I had never been outside the country before — and there were travellers' cheques to negotiate and new clothes to buy.

The organizers of the World Cup had sent us economy-class tickets, but Shearer telephoned me and suggested that we spend the extra money and travel first class. I agreed.

Our Pan-Am flight took us to Los Angeles via Auckland, and while Bob and his manager John Hoare spent the time sleeping and playing backgammon my mind was crowded with too many thoughts to allow sleep. They were old campaigners.

Before we left Sydney airport Shearer assumed the role of senior partner in the team, and I was grateful for his assistance, as he helped me through the formalities that can confuse any first-time overseas traveller. He kept up the father-image role right through our trip together.

I remember clearly when we booked into our hotel at Palm Springs. It was the most palatial establishment I had ever seen, and the huge two-bedroom suite set aside for us took my breath away. It was a far cry from the tiny motel rooms I had shared on the Australian tour just a few weeks earlier.

Shearer watched my reaction with a smile on his face and said, 'Like it, eh'? I was sampling the top life for the first time, and if my skill as a golf player could get me more of it then that is what I wanted. I vowed then that I would travel more, see more and would go first class all the way.

The day after we arrived I was loaned a car for my use during the duration of the World Cup. I found myself at the controls of a left-hand-drive car for the first time in my life. I was sitting behind the wheel on the side where I should be a passenger. The transition was not accomplished without several hair-raising moments, but I got myself to and from the golf club without putting a dent in the vehicle or scratching the duco.

The World Cup that year turned out to be an all-Latin triumph, with the Spanish pair Manuel Pinero and his young partner Severiano Ballesteros beating

the Americans Jerry Pate and Dave Stockton by two shots. The Spaniards scored 574, with Pinero shooting rounds of 75, 70, 72, 68 for 285 and Ballesteros returning 71, 72, 72, 74 for 289.

The individual trophy went to Mexican Ernesto Perez Acosta, three shots clear of Pinero with 69, 74, 69, 70 and a total of 282.

If I had been able to give Shearer more support we would have had a chance of toppling the Spaniards, but my game did not come together as I would have liked and my four rounds of 74, 74, 76, 76 for 300 left me well down the order.

By comparison Shearer shared ninth individual placing after shooting 71, 74, 69, 73 for 287. Shearer's superb golf was the main reason we were able to finish the tournament in a respectable tie for seventh place alongside South Africa.

Spain's victory in the World Cup catapulted Pinero and the younger Ballesteros into national heroes, as it was their country's first victory in the event. Ballesteros had exploded on to the international golf scene earlier in the year, when he had finished joint runner-up to Johnny Miller in the British Open at Royal Birkdale, sharing that spot with Jack Nicklaus. The young Spaniard was being hailed as a future world-beater, and in the next few years we were to play many tournaments against each other.

When Shearer and I had completed our World Cup commitment we allowed ourselves the luxury of a night out at a discothèque, and when we arrived I saw Ballesteros sitting in a corner smoking cigarettes and drinking.

Perhaps he had cause to celebrate, but I said to Shearer, 'Hell. That's not right. A twenty-year-old boy smoking and drinking like that.' I felt disappointed at his attitude.

I heard a great deal about him. We were never introduced to each other during the World Cup matches, but I remember thinking to myself, 'The way he swings the club he can't play. He will bust something sooner or later.'

How wrong I was.

Although our careers took parallel courses from that point, we did not exchange one word for four years. He remained aloof and distant as far as I was concerned. I thought it strange behaviour.

My introduction to the American golf scene and the American life-style left a strong impression on me. Instead of returning to Australia for Christmas as I had originally planned, I stayed on for nearly six weeks as the guest of an American professional I had met in Australia earlier in the year. His name was George Kelly, and his parents owned a house at Pebble Beach near the 13th hole at Spy Glass.

I spent Christmas with the family, and using their home as our base George and I played many of the great courses on the Monterey Peninsula. I also played a round at the Olympic Club in San Francisco where back in 1966 Billy Casper had come from seven shots behind Arnold Palmer with nine to play and made a tie in the U.S. Open. Casper went on to win the play-off next day. My few weeks' holiday in America with George Kelly helped broaden my outlook in many ways. At Pebble Beach one day I was introduced to Clint Eastwood, and we had several long conversations about golf. He was a keen but mediocre player with a genuine interest in the game and the people who played it. I saw him quite often after our original meeting, and found him a basic, down-to-earth guy with a wide range of interests.

George Kelly also introduced me to Doug McClure, whose starring roles in several television series had made him a familiar figure to many thousands of Australians. We met in Sadies Bar in Carmel, not far from the exclusive fish restaurant McClure owned, and several times we were his dinner guests.

When I returned to Australia in mid-January I had one or two tournaments to play, and finished second to Geoff Parslow in the Victorian Open championship at Melbourne's Yarra Yarra Golf Club. But more importantly, I finished ahead of America's Johnny Miller, who had come to Melbourne as the event's celebrity guest. Neither of us looked like catching Parslow, a part-time tournament player, who was also the resident professional at Yarra Yarra. He blitzed the field that year, shooting 63 in one round for a 13 under par total of 275. I was four shots behind him.

Tony Charlton is a former well-known television sports commentator in Australia, but since coming away from in front of the cameras has turned his extraordinary promotional flair to the country's major golf tournaments. When he picked up the flagging Victorian Open he injected several gimmicks into the format which saved the event from obscurity and had the fans flocking to the venue in their thousands.

He brought top women players into the field, and until some pros objected, they played alongside each other. He climaxed the final day of his tournaments by releasing thousands of coloured balloons and having sky-divers parachute on to the 18th green minutes after the last group holed out. They would land to the music of a military band marching up the home fairway. It was colourful stuff, and I know that Miller found the presentation of the tournament a whole lot different to anything he had seen in the United States, or anywhere else for that matter. But apart from the show-biz dimensions he introduced, Charlton runs his tournaments with a style unmatched by anybody in Australia.

After the Victorian Open I had time to sit back and think about the several problems on my mind. The last few months had lifted me to a prominence in golf that I was enjoying, but already I had discovered unexpected and unpleasant pitfalls. I was absolutely naïve in business, and aware that my naïveté could destroy me. I was now twenty-two years old and badly in need of guidance.

It was now nearly six months since my victory at West Lakes, and I was concerned that the company whose equipment I had used had not honoured its agreement. I was entitled to a bonus of $750 for my win, but was told several times by executives of the organization that I would only be paid the bonus money if I entered into a contract with them.

The contract they offered me was a return air ticket to Europe plus $1,500. I told them I would rather die than sign for that amount. 'Unless you do then you will forfeit your bonus for winning West Lakes,' I was told.

As far as I was concerned it was blatant blackmail, and I wanted no part of it. It was the first sour note in a world that otherwise looked rosy.

I had sought advice from Peter Thomson on the way I should pursue 1977 and he was helping me through the formalities of full membership of the PGA which I needed before I could travel overseas.

He was also alert to my other problems. He telephoned me at the suburban motel where I was staying in Melbourne, and told me he was playing at Victoria Golf Club later that day with an Englishman he would like me to meet. 'Join us on the 10th tee,' he suggested.

I arrived in time to watch the group walk through the avenue of trees from the 9th green to the tee, and could not help noticing this stocky figure with a pipe clenched firmly between his teeth.

'Meet James Marshall,' said Thomson. And we shook hands.

I watched the group hit off and walked down the 10th fairway alongside Marshall, discussing the course, the weather, rugby football and generally making small talk.

On the next tee Peter handed me his driver and said, 'Hit one. Show him how good you are.'

I was in street shoes, but with Thomson's driver I let fly with a shot that will stick in my mind for a long time. It split the fairway and soared about 300 yards into the distance.

Marshall was to tell me later that he had never seen a golf-ball hit so far.

I walked the next six holes with Thomson, Marshall and the other member of the group, Guy Wolstenholme, but did not play another shot.

Before I had gone to Victoria Thomson had hinted to me that Marshall was interested in managing a golfer, but was adamant that he had no plans to form a stable along the pattern that the Americans Mark McCormack and Ed Barner operated. I was aware that Marshall had a brilliantly successful business background, not only in England but in the United States and other parts of the world. He invited me to dinner at Melbourne's Hilton Hotel the following night, and keen to pursue the contact further, I accepted.

Marshall probed me about my hopes and aspirations in golf. I told him I hoped to play in Europe and America and that the global tournament scene was my ultimate goal. 'I want to be a great player,' I told him.

I also repeated in detail the unhappy aftermath of my West Lakes victory, and he listened carefully as I spelt out the details and explained how I felt I was being blackmailed. I told him I was stuck in a situation that I did not know how to resolve. Could he help me? 'I can't do anything — I don't manage you. I can't go out there and demand things on your behalf because I'm not legally bound to you,' said Marshall. At that point I asked Marshall whether he would agree to manage me. 'All right. Let's do it,' was his reply.

But there were several conditions upon which he insisted before the legal contract was drawn up between us.

He was adamant that any decision I made about our partnership had to be mine alone. He said he would not undertake the job unless the decision *was* mine alone. 'If you have to go to your family and discuss the whole deal then I want no part of it. The decision has to be yours,' said Marshall. I assured him that was the position, and then James Marshall moved quickly. He asked a Melbourne solicitor to draw up a contract which we both studied carefully, and within forty-eight hours of our dinner together at the Hilton Hotel we signed it. I kept my part of the bargain. I discussed my plans with nobody, and we signed the contract on 17 February 1977.

I felt I had grown up. I had made the biggest decision of my life. I soon learned why Marshall had insisted on my complete autonomy in the negotiations. He had been interested in helping the young British player Nick Faldo in a managerial role, but quickly shelved the idea when Faldo's family wanted to become involved.

The people closest to me were bewildered by the speed of my move. I had placed myself in the hands of a man who was a complete stranger to them. They were all anxious to meet this pipe-smoking Englishman who was to have such a profound influence on my future, and during that week in Melbourne I introduced them. I had made my judgment, and that was that. The fact that Marshall was a close friend of both Peter Thomson and Guy Wolstenholme was a big factor in my decision. They were men of substance, and so was Marshall.

My parents, Charlie Earp and the captain of Royal Queensland Golf Club, Doug Cranstoun, were all in Melbourne at the time. To say they were flabbergasted at my new move was putting it mildly. They all had my best interests at heart, and were demanding more information about this English intruder into their circle.

I remember vividly (and with a chuckle) the time I was discussing our plans with Marshall when the phone rang in his hotel room and it was Charlie Earp on the other end of the line, demanding to know Marshall's credentials and his aspirations for the new partnership.

And obviously Charlie was being blunt and very forthright.

Marshall's eyebrows shot up at one stage of the conversation, and with all his

English dignity he said, 'Don't you swear at me, Charles.'

Within a fortnight the bonus cheque of $750 due to me from the West Lakes Classic was in my bank.

Marshall and I developed a close rapport in the intervening years, and if it had not been for his guidance and managerial skills I would not be in the sound position I am today. His social and business contacts opened more doors for me than I would have dreamed possible. He instilled in me a more gracious, more worldly and more sophisticated approach to life, and I am sure time laid to rest any fear that my parents or friends had when we forged that link in Melbourne.

Marshall's business reputation spreads through most of the world, and he is a recognized expert in the area of company partnerships. For many years he was on the board of a Rolls-Royce subsidiary. Few people know that he worked as a stevedore in Canada, and that he saw active service in Malaysia as a lieutenant in the British Army. There is an autocratic air about the man that commands respect. People listen to him, and he is a forceful debater when it is time to negotiate a business deal. His acumen comes from many years around board tables. Sometimes I felt he was possessive, that he took a personal pride in the moulding of Greg Norman, and if that was the way he felt then I understand.

I do not underestimate the influence he has had on my life.

CHAPTER 9
BRITISH DEBUT

With James Marshall in control of my career it started moving along a well-defined path.

Despite the extraordinary success I had enjoyed through the latter months of 1976 (culminating in my selection in the World Cup) I was in a quandary about where to head next. I was determined that I would not spend the year in Australia looking for minor pickings. I felt my golf was at the point where it had to be tested in a bigger league, and my eyes were set on England and Europe.

Marshall and I spent many hours plotting an itinerary that would get me to England in time to play the major tournaments leading up to that year's British Open at Turnberry, Scotland.

The Australian Golf Writers Association voted me the outstanding young player of the year following my 1976 success, and with that acknowledgment went a return ticket to England donated by McCallum's Whisky. As a fledgling pro, undecided in which direction to turn, that award helped me plot a course. I will always be grateful for their early support.

Marshall's global business interests spread into Japan, and through his contacts in that country he obtained invitations for me to play in three tournaments before heading to England for the first time.

He made arrangements for me to travel with Guy Wolstenholme, who was also heading for the same series of events, and once again the rookie traveller was well chaperoned on his first visit to the Orient.

My first tournament was at Nagoya in the Kuzaha Open over the 'sprint' course of 36 holes, and when I finished with a 5 under par total I pocketed the first prize and left behind a stunned field of the best players in Japan.

It was an exciting introduction to Japan, and my win focused enormous publicity on me. It also helped me secure a foothold in Japan in future years, and I looked forward keenly to my annual visit to that country. In the past two decades the Japanese tour has developed into a lucrative arena for professional golfers, and invitations to play there are keenly sought after.

I performed reasonably well in the next tournament, but missed the cut in the Chunichi Crowns before flying out to England.

Marshall was there to meet me at Heathrow airport in his big black Bentley. It was freezing cold, and with my first English tournament only a few days away my first priority was to buy some warm clothes.

I fell in love with Beaurepaire House the minute Marshall turned the big

Bentley into the long driveway and eased to a stop at the front entrance. If it was not one of England's stately homes, then it was the next best thing in my eyes. It was to be my English home for long periods, and as soon as we unpacked I wandered through the spacious gardens and explored every corner of the old manor. 'Do you like it?' asked Marshall, in a question loaded with pride of ownership. 'It is beautiful, absolutely beautiful,' I replied.

James Marshall lives in grand style, and likes to do things in a grand manner. He has now moved from Beaurepaire House into an equally beautiful home in the Gloucestershire village of Sapperton. It is set in huge, immaculately kept gardens, where the hedges have been trimmed in exactly the same way for four hundred years. The Prince and Princess of Wales have a home a few miles away, and the area is at the heart of England's polo-playing country, and dotted with the estates of many of its most wealthy people.

It is only a few years ago that the moat which once surrounded Beaurepaire House was filled in. Shortly after Marshall, his wife Lois and Marshall's chauffeur-cum-manservant David moved in, an accident occurred which sounded the death-knell of that centuries-old-ditch. Marshall had installed an oil-heating system to warm his comfortable old home, and one day the bridge over the moat collapsed under the weight of the truck delivering the fuel. It took two days to drag the truck clear.

A few days after I had settled in Marshall and I were off to Royal St George's at Sandwich for my first taste of the British professional tour.

We were back home in Beaurepaire House much more quickly than I expected, as I missed the cut with a couple of very forgettable rounds. Including my failure in the Chunichi Crowns before I flew to England, I had now missed two cuts in successive tournaments, and I wondered whether my new English manager thought he had become involved with a 'lemon'.

After every tournament I play, win or lose, I go over it with a mental microscope, trying to determine where I made the mistakes, and whether my errors were in shot-making or in thinking. They are private post-mortems which I seldom share with anybody.

I had plenty to ponder over in the next few days at Beaurepaire House before setting off once again — this time to the Martini International tournament at Blairgowrie. I had already excused my failure at Royal St George's on two grounds — one that it was so cold I could hardly hold my club, and the other that I just did not think the course suited me.

I have played the course several times since, including the British Open in 1981, and my mind has not changed. I dislike the type of golf test Royal St George's presents because I believe luck plays too great a part. I dislike St Andrews and Muirfield for the same reason, and if my many British friends believe I am indulging in heresy I hope they will forgive me.

Maybe it is because I have not played well on those courses that I express this opinion, but I think my type of golf is best suited to layouts like Wentworth, where I have been successful. Of the coastal courses I prefer Portmarnock in Ireland, and I do like Royal Birkdale. But up to now there are several of the famous links layouts in Britain on which I have not played, so I will reserve judgment on them.

I prefer to play 'target' golf on a course where I know that there is no hidden pimple in the middle of the fairway to send my ball into strangling rough.

It is a matter of opinion. Many players agree with me, many do not.

It took me several years of playing in the United Kingdom to form these opinions, so none of them were in my mind when I drove to Blairgowrie. A couple of practice rounds over the course with its birch- and heather-lined fairways and I immediately felt more comfortable than I had at Royal St George's. Deep down I was confident and eager for the event to start.

The field was a good one, with the Rhodesian Simon Hobday and myself giving it an international flavour, and the best of the British tourists all in the firing-line.

Yorkshireman Howard Clark fired three rounds of 69, 70, 70 to lead into the last round, and I was happily positioned two shots behind him with three rounds of 70, 71, 70.

The fireworks started in the final round, and after reaching the turn in 34 I was

Striding out with Nick Faldo during the 1978 Euro Open at Walton Heath, England.

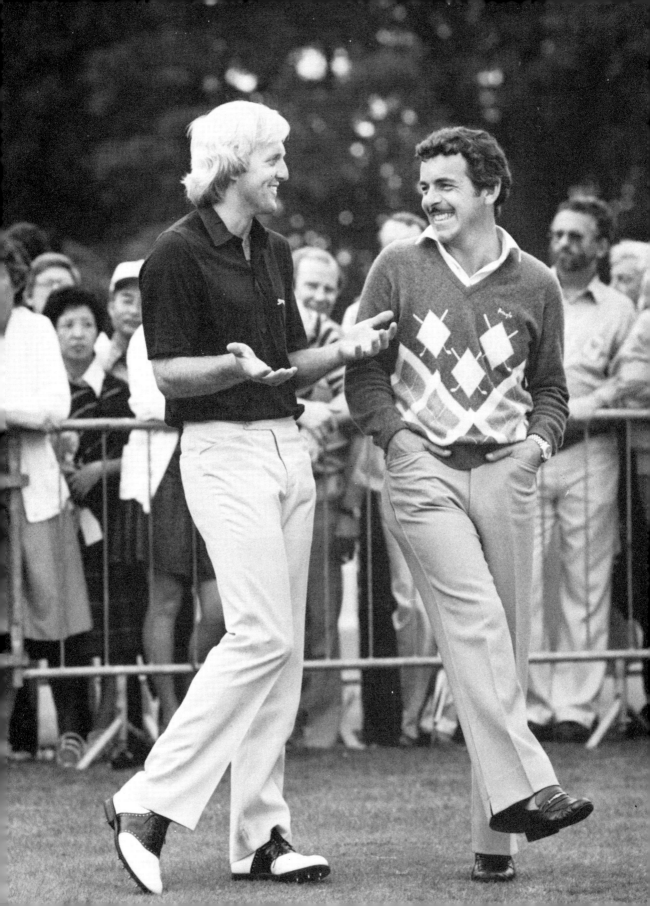

still just two shots behind the tenacious Clark.

I birdied three holes in succession from the 10th, parred the 13th and then birdied the 14th and 15th to go 12 under par for the tournament and four shots clear of the field.

I came home in 32, and my final round of 66 set a new course record for Blairgowrie and gave me a three-shot winning margin over Hobday.

My four-round total of 277 was 11 under par.

I had good reason to be satisfied. 'Dazzler Greg storms in' was how the *Sunday Express* acclaimed my first victory in England, and their golf correspondent Ronald Heager was moved to comment about my five birdies in six holes .... 'It swept him to a £3000 victory in only his second appearance in Britain, and the big blond they call the Australian Jack Nicklaus lived up to that tag with a show of power and precision.' The London *Sunday Telegraph* said :

> The day belonged to Norman who must be the most exciting newcomer to hit the world professional scene for some considerable time. Norman catches both the eye and the imagination. With his blond hair and Nicklaus hairstyle goes a lovely looping swing and a slide into the ball that generates enormous power with no apparent effort. Just like Nicklaus he hits it very high.

My twenty-second birthday was only four months behind me. I had now won three tournaments in three different countries, and could it be only ten months ago that I walked out of Charlie Earp's pro shop at Royal Queensland 'on trial' as an invited trainee?

It seemed like light-years ago.

My Martini victory was to prove a potent weapon in the hands of James Marshall, who had already opened business talks with the giant Wilson Sporting Goods company in America. After we had spent a few days back at Beaurepaire House, Marshall came to see me and said, 'Pack a bag. We are off to Los Angeles. The Wilson people want to talk to us.'

I had been well aware of the preliminary talks Marshall had held, but could not imagine why they would be interested in a relatively unknown player from Australia. On the flight across the Atlantic, Marshall explained to me why he had asked me to join him in the talks with Wilson. He was painfully aware of my business innocence, and said he wanted to involve me in the negotiations so I could see how it all worked.

By the time we left the United States for the trip home I held a three-year contract with the Wilson company worth $100,000 plus bonuses. I sat through the negotiations alongside Marshall, and as he predicted, I was intrigued by the parry and thrust that went on across the conference table.

When I walked into the discussions alongside Marshall the Wilson executives with whom we were negotiating looked startled.

'It is the first time we have had a player at these sort of talks,' they said.

The Greg Norman-James Marshall partnership was off to a flying start.

Opposite
Weighing-up the prospects with Tony Jacklin during the 1982 Euro Open at Sunningdale, England.

CHAPTER 10
OVER THE WATER

Bruno and Celia became very close friends of mine. They were the two German Shepherd dogs Marshall kept as pets at Beaurepaire House, and with them I spent many relaxing hours hunting in the Hampshire woods. After my first Martini victory Marshall had presented me with a magnificent 'under and over' shotgun, and whenever I had spare time I would take the dogs with me and stalk through the woods in search of game.

Sometimes I would spend four or five hours wandering through the forests alone with the dogs, and if we did not sight any prey then I was not concerned. I like to be alone, and I found those walks a great escape from the hustle and bustle and the tensions of the tournament scene.

Most times the hunting was a minor consideration when compared with the solitude I found. Bruno was a born hunter, and would trot ahead of me, sometimes flushing out a rabbit or a hare, while Celia stuck by my side.

And all the time I was soaking up the atmosphere and life-style of Beaurepaire House, finding new values, meeting new people and appreciating a broader canvas.

Whenever possible I used Beaurepaire House as my home base if the tournaments were within driving distance. I was always anxious to return there, take out my shotgun from the closet and set out into the woods with the dogs.

During my time at Beaurepaire House I met James Marshall's identical twin brother John, whose entrepreneurial flair matched his brother's. John had just returned from the United States, where he produced the film *The Greatest*, the life-story of the incomparable Muhammad Ali. Ali was in London for the film première, and I was invited along with James and his wife Lois. I was looking forward eagerly to meeting the great fighter.

A huge crowd jostled for positions outside the cinema as the celebrities arrived, and when Ali stepped from his car he waved and joked with them as the invited guests moved inside. After the première showing he hosted a glittering champagne party in his suite at the Hilton Hotel, where John Marshall called him away from his admirers and introduced us. 'You enjoy that movie'? he asked, and I assured him I had. I saw quite a lot of Ali after that, and found him a strange mixture of a man, similar in many ways to Lee Trevino. Publicly he was an extrovert, always ready with a quick word or a joke, but in private he was very much the opposite.

One night, shortly after the film had been launched, John Marshall hosted a

small dinner party to which James, his wife and myself were invited. Like James, John enjoyed the good life, and Hyfield House in the village of Heckfield matched the taste and style of Beaurepaire House.

Ali and his wife Veronica were house guests of John and Elizabeth Marshall, but when the seven of us sat down for dinner a strange routine began. Ali and his wife ate their meal just one course ahead of the rest of us, and as hostess Elizabeth was kept on her toes. There was no sign of the wisecracking, the quick aside or the smart banter usually associated with 'The Greatest', and it was an odd experience.

Before the rest of us started our main course Ali and his wife excused themselves and went upstairs to bed. They had hardly spoken a word during the course of the meal.

I found his attitude difficult to reconcile, particularly as he was a guest in the house of not only one of his closest friends but also an intimate business associate.

But earlier in the day it had been a different story. With the Marshall twins Ali and I drove to the village pub — the New Inn — owned by a good friend of mine, Basil Francis, whose eyebrows shot up as we walked through the door.

A few drinks at the local in the village of Heckfield, England. John Marshall (*left*) is the identical twin brother of my former manager James and produced the film *The Greatest*. And that is James doing the talking. Muhammad Ali drank orange juice.

69

The few customers in the bar quickly recognized Ali as we ordered our drinks. He sipped an orange juice as we drank our lagers. We stayed for three or four drinks, and when we walked out to the car-park to return home it was crowded with the villagers and their children.

The word had spread like a bushfire that Muhammad Ali was in the village, and having a drink at the local. Within seconds he was surrounded by his excited fans, wanting to touch him, and pushing their autograph books at him. He sparred with the kids, talked and joked with their parents and for ten minutes the car-park at Heckfield's local pub was turned into a stage.

It was Ali at his best, and that little corner of England will never forget him.

James and I were to see Ali again later that year, when the amazing likeness between the two Marshall brothers was to leave him bewildered. We were in Los Angeles on business and just leaving the Beverley Wiltshire Hotel for an appointment. As we came out of the hotel doors Ali turned his big white convertible Rolls-Royce into the driveway of the hotel. He spotted us immediately, and yelled across the intervening forty yards, 'Hey, John. How are you'?

He waved excitedly, and as we drove away he was obviously convinced that James was John. It had happened before. The likeness is quite extraordinary.

My last glimpse of Ali was as he drove slowly away through the large throng that had surrounded his Rolls-Royce in the minute or so he had stopped. Perhaps he is still wondering why 'John' Marshall did not pause for a chat.

The Wilson contract Marshall had successfully negotiated for me the year before paved the way to an extravagance I had never been able to enjoy previously. I had carefully stored away the tournament winnings from my victories in Australia, Japan and England, but backed by my new contract the frugality I had practised in Australia was about to be replaced by a spending splurge.

One day I said to James, 'Come into London with me. I want to buy some new clothes.'

'I know just the place and just the man to see,' said Marshall.

Before we left Beaurepaire House he telephoned the manager of one of London's leading stores and then we set off on the biggest shopping spree I have ever indulged in.

A new dinner suit, slacks, shirts, sports coats, jackets, suits, shoes, underwear, ties — the whole magnificent range. I bought freely but carefully, with the store manager at one elbow advising me and James at the other.

A new watch to go with it all, and I walked out of the store completely re-equipped — and $7,000 lighter in pocket. The whole expedition had taken several hours. I had not bought indiscriminately.

Perhaps the original decision had been impetuous, but I do not regret a minute or a cent of it. In my profession, I believe smart dressing is one of our trademarks, and I enjoy the fact that I stand out. If I am supposed to be making a lot of money on the golf tour, then I want to look as if I am. I believe the golf fans relate to us better when they see their favourite players turned out in well-cut, good-quality clothes, while feeling just right on a golf-course can help you play better. Or I believe it does.

My Wilson contract and my tournament earnings were giving me a new slant on life, a new feeling of security and prosperity. But not once did I allow it to

70

interfere with my dedication towards playing golf ... because I understood clearly that my new standing also gave me an added responsibility towards the people who had shown faith in me. And I was determined to justify that faith.

I have put the sports-car image behind me.

The money — and the temptations — were there, and my shopping splurge was followed quickly by another. This time I bought a gleaming red Ferrari.

My red Ferrari and fair hair became all too familiar as I sped along the M4, at times way above the speed-limit, but thrilling to the very power of the machine under me.

The little village of Bramley Green was not far from Beaurepaire House, and I always stopped for my petrol at the local garage, where the mechanics regularly inquired, 'How's she running, chum'?

I love talking cars and their relative performances, and would often dwell too long chatting to my friends at the Bramley Green garage when I should have been on my way to either Wentworth or Sunningdale.

My joy of the open road was earning me a certain notoriety around Hampshire, and I dare say my luck had to run out. It did. I was booked for speeding — the police said I was doing 112 mph and I don't query it — and subsequently fined.

Several times I played hide-and-seek with the police, dodging off the main highway and reaching Beaurepaire House by a more roundabout route. A few days after I had been booked I was due to fly to America to compete in the World

Series of Golf, so I arranged for a solicitor to represent me at the court hearing.

I returned home to discover I had been fined £150.

After a time I decided that my red Ferrari was far too conspicuous, so I put it in the garage and went out and bought a silver Ferrari ... this time a more powerful GTS model.

Once, on an open stretch of road, I pushed it to 162 mph.

I was only stopped once for speeding in the GTS, and the policeman asked me for my autograph and let me go with a stern warning. I was flattered. I did not even ask him if he played golf.

When my close friend and fellow pro golfer Stewart Ginn stayed at Beaurepaire House with the Marshalls on one of his visits to England I took the red car out of moth-balls and loaned it to him. Strange, he has hair nearly as fair as mine, but he was never caught speeding!

The whole era is behind me now, and I can reflect on it without any regrets. I now drive sedate sedans within the speed-limit, and never fear glancing in the rear vision mirror. Although the ownership of two Ferraris may seem like a vulgar extravagance one must remember that they were also solid investments.

It was into the traditionally English environment of Beaurepaire House that I introduced my fiancée Laura Andrassy in mid-1979.

The romance that was to lead to marriage just two years later started as Marshall and I were flying back from Detroit to New York in June 1979. I had just played my first American Open at Inverness, and was well satisfied with my top 25 finish.

Immediately I spotted the stewardess welcoming us aboard our America Airlines flight I turned to Marshall and said, 'I would like to meet her. What a nice-looking girl!'

The flying-time to New York was only forty minutes, just time for a few drinks, but for once in my life I was delighted when traffic congestion over La Guardia Airport kept us aloft for an extra forty minutes.

There were very few people travelling first class on the flight, and when Marshall and I ordered drinks it was Laura who brought them to us.

In his most gallant manner Marshall stood up from his aisle seat, introduced me as 'Gregory Norman' (which I dislike) and almost pushed Laura into the seat alongside me. Then in total contravention of the rules my manager went along to the galley and helped the other girls mix drinks while Laura and I chatted.

I talked fast. The traffic hold-up had given me extra time to get to know this charming lass, and I intended to put it to good use.

'Will you have dinner with me when the flight lands?'

'Oh, no. It will be far too late,' she said.

I told her I was catching a 6.00 a.m. flight to Bermuda next morning, where I had to play an exhibition match.

'Would you join me for a late drink?'

'Oh, no. It will be far too late,' she repeated.

'Can I call you when I get to my hotel?'

I persisted, and as our flight continued its circling Laura finally changed her mind and agreed to have dinner with me.

It was nearly midnight when we touched down.

When Marshall and I arrived at our hotel I told him I was taking the young lady out for dinner. He looked sceptical.

While we were in the hotel lobby checking in, over the paging system came the message 'Telephone call for Mr Gregory Norman, telephone call for Mr Gregory Norman.'

I grabbed the phone from the reception desk, and was overjoyed to hear Laura on the other end of the line.

'Hi. We are stuck at the airport. There is a petrol shortage in New York and we cannot get a taxi. I will be another hour before I get into town.'

I threw my bags into my room and went downstairs looking for a cab. Laura's hotel was nearly an hour's drive across town, and there was not a cab in sight. I was standing outside the hotel cursing my luck and the New York petrol shortage when a black limousine pulled up and its two passengers alighted and went inside the hotel.

I ran around to the driver's side, put my head through the window and asked, 'Are you free now?'

'Sure, man. Jump in,' said the Negro driver.

I felt like the President of the United States as I sat in the back seat, speeding across town to keep a date that was destined to change my life.

It was nearly 1.00 a.m. when Laura joined me in the back seat of the limousine. 'I don't know New York at all. You will have to be our guide,' I told her. And in high spirits we set out to find a quiet place for a drink and a meal.

'Sorry. We have just called for last drinks and are about to close' we were told at our first stop. We tried two more restaurants, and got the same answer. Even the Playboy Club was closing.

Both of us could see the amusing side of the situation and we had plenty of laughs — but no food and no drink. At 3.00 a.m. we admitted defeat and I dropped Laura back at her hotel, determined to see her again but wondering whether I ever would.

By the time I returned to my hotel the bill for the limousine had soared to $200.

'You are crazy,' said Marshall.

I had time for only a couple of hours' sleep before hurrying to the airport early next morning for the flight to Bermuda. I played the exhibition match, but it was a round of golf on which I found it difficult to concentrate.

My thoughts were back in New York ... and with Laura. I kept wondering when I would see her again. When our Bermuda commitment was finished Marshall and I flew back to England and Beaurepaire House, where I planned to spend a few days before heading to Tokyo and two tournaments in Japan. On the flight across the Atlantic I thought a great deal about Laura, and told Marshall I was determined to see her again. Before leaving for Japan I phoned her several times. 'You're wasting your money,' said Marshall.

When I reached Japan almost the first thing I did was call Laura. I told her I planned to change my flight and go to London via New York, and although she sounded incredulous at my 'shuttle courting', she agreed to see me.

We spent all day together, and that night enjoyed dinner together in the moonlight at the Twin Trade Towers restaurant, and it was a meal that lingered long into the evening. We were getting to know each other.

Laura's knowledge of golf and the people who played it would have filled a thimble. It was only because Jack Nicklaus and Arnold Palmer were household names that she knew of them.

On an impulse I asked her to fly to England for the British Open due to be played in a month at Royal Lytham and St Anne's. She refused. Later she was to confide to her friends, 'The guy must be crazy. I have only known him for two days and he has asked me to go to England.' When I returned to England I continued to try to persuade her to come over to the Open, but she said, 'The tournament is too important to you and I would only be in the way.'

But she did agree to fly across when the Open had finished. In the meantime I sent her two dozen red roses for her birthday. I was in love.

CHAPTER 11
THE HONG KONG OPEN

I won four tournaments in Australia and one in Fiji during 1978, with a three-shot victory in the New South Wales Open the most important. I got to within one shot of the record set by Jack Nicklaus for Sydney's Manly layout, shooting a course record 64 in the opening round and following it up with 72, 69, 70. My total of 275 was 13 under par, and three shots better than Billy Dunk, with Bob Shearer in third place on 282.

Earlier in the year I had come from behind to win the Festival of Sydney tournament at The Lakes Golf Club, setting a new course record of 64 in the final round.

My other wins included the South Seas Classic around the very testing Robert Trent Jones course at Fiji's Pacific Harbour holiday resort, and I also won the Traralgon Classic from a solid local field in Victoria.

Any win is a good win in the world of professional golf, but although I was elated with these victories the major championships of the Australian tour eluded me.

Nicklaus came and conquered at The Australian Golf Club later in the year, winning his sixth Australian Open, while his countryman Hale Irwin took our PGA title back to America with a brilliant performance at Royal Melbourne.

Irwin was unbeatable that week, winning by eight strokes from Graham Marsh. His opening round of 64 over the majestic Royal Melbourne composite course still stands as a record, and despite being headed by Marsh at the halfway stage the American ran away with the tournament.

Their relative scoring is interesting. Irwin shot 64, 75, 70, 69 for 278, while Marsh went 71, 66, 74, 75 for 286. Seve Ballesteros finished third, while I was in a group alongside Bruce Devlin, Johnny Miller and Roger Davis on 291 and a share of fourth place.

When Nicklaus came to Sydney he came as the spearhead of the biggest American invasion for our Open in history. He had been retained by Australian television magnate Kerry Packer to redesign the layout of The Australian Golf Club in a deal that soared past the $1 million dollar mark but turned the course into a superb golf test.

Packer was also the joint sponsor to the tournament, and it was common knowledge in golf circles that he was backing the Australian Open for the last time. Under Packer's sponsorship the Australian Golf Union was convinced it

Ready to cast off aboard
Divot II.

was losing control of its biggest tournament 'plum'. Many of the Union members were unhappy with Packer's domination of the event.

Nicklaus had not yet put the finishing touches to the reconstruction of the course when the 1978 title was played there, and America's veteran tourist Miller Barber was one man who said feelingly, 'The course is too new for a major championship.'

New or not, Nicklaus set about taming his own handiwork with rounds of 73, 66, 74, 71 to win by a mammoth six shots from countryman Ben Crenshaw, and his total of 284 was the only score under par, and indeed, under 290. Six Americans finished in the top seven places, with only Graham Marsh on 295 and fourth place interrupting their domination. In the circumstances my total of 300 was fair golf, but like everybody else I missed many opportunities. Perhaps Miller Barber was right.

Early in 1979 Marshall and I agreed that I should go to the East for the Hong Kong Open sponsored by Cathay Pacific Airways, with whom Marshall was considering a business link.

As it turned out I won the championship at my first attempt, but before I accepted the winner's cheque and the huge trophy that went with the title there were many worrying moments ... not all of them on the golf course.

It was touch and go whether I made it to the tee in time for the last round.

Anybody who has ever made the long drive from the city to the Royal Hong Kong Golf Club at Fanling will appreciate the dilemma in which I found myself on the final day of the tournament. It is a drive that is never measured in miles — only time. On a good day the distance can be covered in an hour and a half.

On a bad day — well, I struck one, and it took just over three hours.

The highway is the only main road servicing the New Territories from Hong

Kong, and at weekends it is packed with traffic as the residents of the city head for picnic outings in the country. The car taking me to Fanling for the final round of the tournament became hopelessly caught up in the worst traffic jam I have ever encountered. As we edged along in low gear, bumper to bumper and still many miles from the golf course, I glanced at my watch. My manager James Marshall was sitting in the back seat alongside me, and when I said, 'We are going to be lucky to make it' he nodded in agreement.

We both cursed the traffic, and then sat back and relaxed.

There was really no point in getting into a panic. I normally like an hour on the practice fairway and putting green before a tournament round, but I knew I had no chance of that luxury.

We had a bare five minutes to spare when our car turned into the driveway of the golf-club. I had already changed into my golf-shoes, and had just enough time to hit three wedge shots down the practice fairway before I was called to the tee.

My playing partner was the talented Lu Hsi-chuen, or 'Little Lu', a nephew of the great Taiwanese player Lu Liang-huan or, as he is known throughout the golf world, 'Mr Lu'.

The Royal Hong Kong Golf Club, situated just a few miles from the border of Red China, embodies all the traditions of the great British clubs, while the three courses it controls are named after those at St Andrews — the Old, the New and the Eden.

On the first two days of the tournament we played alternately on the New and the Eden, and for the final 36 holes we played a composite of both.

My countryman Graham Marsh had set a scorching pace over the first two days, shooting 66 over the New course and following it up the next day with a 65 over the Eden. He played breath-taking golf, knocking the flag out with his iron shots and ramming home his putts.

I had opened with a 70 and followed it with 66 on the Eden course to be well satisfied with my position, although spotting Graham Marsh five shots was a task that looked formidable.

It was not so much the pressure from behind him that brought about Marsh's undoing on the crucial third day. He got off on the wrong foot at the very first hole, driving his ball behind a tree en-route to a six-bogey 74 and a rapid slide from leadership.

I picked up an eagle at the long 12th hole on my way to a 69, caught Marsh, but was still three strokes adrift of the lead now shared by Little Lu and Hsu Chi-san. They had both returned third rounds of 69 and were on 202, while my 54-hole total was 205.

I was drawn with Little Lu in the final pairing for the last round, and when I walked onto the tee I wondered if he was aware of the problems I had met just to get there. If he wasn't, then I was not about to tell him.

When I saw the size of the gallery around the opening hole I quickly realized why we had experienced so much difficulty in getting to the course. The Chinese love their sport, and a huge gallery had come to Fanling for the climax of the four-day battle. By the end of the day most of them were around myself and Little Lu as the championship came down to a two-man affair.

Lu reminds me of an Asiatic Gary Player. He is a stocky, broad-shouldered young man and like the South African gives the ball a powerful thump. In fact, this Hong Kong Open was only his second tournament as a professional, and he was striving gallantly to continue the run of victories the Taiwanese had enjoyed in the event for the previous five years.

Like Player, he prefers to dress in all-black.

Although I was three behind as we headed into the final round, the tournament started to swing my way far quicker than I would have dared hope. A couple of bogeys from Lu and back-to-back birdies from me at the 3rd and 4th holes, and I was a shot in front.

Early in the final round Marsh and Hsu ran into their share of bogeys and Lu and I were left to resolve the championship virtually by match-play. And it was easy to tell where the crowd's sympathies lay.

As the *South China Morning Post* reported, 'Lu had quite vociferous support … the shouts and cheers echoed around the tree fringed green …

Without question an incident at the 9th hole turned the crowd against me and more firmly behind Lu.

I was still nursing the one-shot lead I had earned with my birdie at the 4th when we reached the halfway hole, where my second shot kicked through the back of the green. Because I would be forced to stand in defined GUR to play my next shot I asked for, and got, relief.

We waited several minutes for Mr Tony Webb, a member of the tournament committee, to arrive, and when he ruled in my favour the predominantly Chinese crowd were vocally annoyed. It was the sort of incident one rarely sees on a golf-course. The boisterous crowd and the long delay at the 9th were hardly the right ingredients to soothe the nerves, and the final few holes were packed with tension. Both of us made our share of errors as the championship moved to its climax, and when Lu parred the 16th and my second shot found a greenside trap and I bogeyed, there was only a shot separating us.

I stood on the final tee still nursing a one-shot lead, and punched my second shot 14 feet from the hole with Lu just on the edge. Barring accidents, I knew I had won then, but I felt a twinge of sadness for Lu when his lag putt finished 7 feet away and he missed it. That final three-putt green robbed him of outright second place, pushing him back into a tie with Hsu and Chen Tse-ming.

For the pro-Lu crowd I turned the finish into something of an anticlimax by holing my birdie putt, and eventually winning by three shots after a final round of 68.

It was my first experience on the Asian tour, and surviving the last-round dog-fight against Little Lu had brought me my biggest prize ever since turning professional — $20,000. The trauma at the 9th hole was unnerving, but in retrospect it did not match the trauma of just getting to Fanling for the final round.

I can do without that sort of distraction.

Perhaps the most surprising aspect of the tournament was Marsh's fall from grace after his superb opening two rounds. For a player of his undoubted class it was sad to see him surrender so quickly, and his closing round of 76 sent him tumbling down the order into seventh place. It was certainly not the true Graham Marsh.

The prophecies made about the potential of Little Lu were borne out in the next couple of tournaments on the Asian tour, as he won the Singapore Open after two holes of overtime against Hsu Sheng-san and the Malaysian Open a week later. At Royal Selangor he 'streeted' the opposition, winning by seven shots from the American Ron Milanovich with four rounds of 69, 71, 67, 70 for a total of 277.

Like most of the Taiwanese, Little Lu has a masterly short game to complement an extremely accurate long game, and his rookie year on the Asian circuit was nothing short of sensational. Like his illustrious uncle, he is destined for great things.

I have been a regular competitor in the Hong Kong Open since my successful first appearance there, and believe the Asian circuit deserves the support it gets from Australia's leading tournament professionals. There are many highly skilled players in the world who prefer to compete on tournament circuits away from the cutthroat atmosphere of the U.S. tour, and Asia is one of the more lucrative and more pleasant alternatives.

There is no question that just getting to Fanling poses its problems, or perhaps I am jinxed. In 1982 the Rolls-Royce in which I was being driven to the course was involved in an accident, but I was lucky enough to hail a cab on the crowded highway, and made my tee-time quite comfortably. Such is life.

The Martini International is a tournament that has treated me kindly in my British and European campaigns, but after my opening round of the event in 1979 the chances of a Greg Norman win were as bleak as the weather.

You will recall that my first win on British soil was in the 1977 Martini tournament — and in fact I had not won in England since then.

In 1979 the tournament brought together the best talent of the European tour, headed by Seve Ballesteros, Brian Barnes, Tony Jacklin, Neil Coles and Ken Brown. At the end of a soggy, dismal week where the scoring generally matched the miserable weather pattern, my four-round total was a level-par 288, and it is not often level par is good enough to win. On this occasion it was — thankfully.

Wentworth is universally referred to as the 'Burma Road' because of its punishing final three holes, but they are holes that suit me because of my length advantage over most players from the tee. After opening the tournament with a mediocre 75 which left me trailing the first-round leader John Morgan by six shots, I virtually set up my success with 67 in the second round. It was the lowest score of the week.

It was a week quite a few players would like to forget, because very few tournaments produce the bizarre sideshows of the 1979 Martini International.

Brian Barnes is one of the most jovial characters in professional golf, but even his good humour turned sour. He arrived six minutes late for his tee-time in the third round, and hit off in his street shoes, but when he was told at the fourth hole that he had incurred a two-shot penalty his reaction was quite out of character. In sheer anger he picked up a tee marker and hurled it over the fence into a next-door garden. 'They could have waited until I had finished,' growled Barnes.

Until that blow-up Barnes had been right in the firing-line with openers of 75-69, but his shattered composure sent him soaring to a third round of 79 and firmly in the ruck.

I could not help chuckling when I saw the official version of Brian's 'blow-up' in the Press tent. 'He had been seen to react unfavourably' was a gem of an understatement.

Then Neil Coles missed a putt of one inch. Can you imagine? Poor Coles went

to tap in his ball, but instead stubbed the putter behind it.

Nobody will ever know what Francisco Abreu made at this particular hole. Francisco is a former arm-wrestling champion from the Canary Islands, and plays his golf out of Tenerife. He probably headed back there after taking four (or was it five?) putts from three feet, still without holing out! He said 'Thank you' to his marker, picked up his ball and disappeared.

But back to the golf tournament.

The final thirty-six holes were played in one day, and my playing partner was the Royal Liverpool professional John Morgan, who was a shot ahead of me when we teed off. Because of his club responsibilities Morgan had been on the tour for only two full years, and the hopes of a British victory were squarely on his shoulders.

I returned a level par 72 in the third round to Morgan's 74, and took a one-shot lead into the final 18 holes. By the time we reached the final hole — a long dog-leg — we were aware that the Spaniard Antonio Garrido had posted a 73, and was in the clubhouse on 289.

It was an intriguing situation. If I could make a birdie I would win, but if I parred the hole and Morgan birdied then we would be in a three-way tie with Garrido.

My tee shot was tucked in a little close to the tree-line, but I cracked a 3-wood for my second, which faded perfectly into the green. I left myself a 7-footer for the birdie and the title, and anybody who has faced a putt of that length will understand the strain.

Morgan was only three feet from the hole for his birdie, and must have had mixed emotions as I went through my lining-up routine. Once I had selected the line I gave the ball a firm rap and it found the target.

I had won. Whatever happened to Morgan's 3-footer could not alter that fact, and I was relieved for him when he tapped it in for a share of second place with Garrido.

The British Press made great play of my 'double Martini', and even if the scoring had been below the standard expected from the purists the weather was the biggest contributor to that situation. It was still only May, and with two wins to my credit for the year I was looking forward keenly to the campaigns ahead.

The British Open was set down that year for one of Britain's most demanding courses, Royal Lytham and St Anne's close by the famous old seaside resort of Blackpool. It was not a course with which I was very familiar. My victory at Wentworth had been my tenth since I first set out as a professional golfer just three years earlier, and for every young player the Open is the ultimate achievement.

Dare I think about it?

When I drove back to Beaurepaire House from Wentworth that evening I picked up my shotgun from the closet, and with Bruno and Celia wandered through the forest in the lingering twilight.

There were many things to ponder over.

My golf was reaching a maturity where youthful dreams of victory in one of the world's major championships was a real possibility.

I resolved to take off the week before the Open and play Lytham as often as I could. I wanted to get to know the place like the back of my hand.

'Do you agree, Bruno?' I asked as we turned for the walk home. And he wagged his tail approvingly.

CHAPTER 12
TEMPER AND TEMPERAMENT

The day after the British Open had finished at Royal Lytham and St Anne's I drove my red Ferrari to Heathrow airport to meet Laura. I arrived well before the flight landed, and sat down with a cup of coffee and read the morning newspapers. It had been only four weeks since I had first met her, but during that time she had dominated my thoughts.

I was anxious to see her again. She had never visited England before, and I was keenly looking forward to showing her as much as I could in the short time she was to be in the UK.

As the passengers streamed out of the baggage collection area I scanned their faces closely, but there was no sign of Laura. Had she changed her mind at the last minute and decided not to come?

As the flow of people started to slacken my concern grew.

By sheer coincidence Sydney newspaperman Tom Ramsey (who was in England covering the golf tour) was at Heathrow waiting to catch a flight back to Australia.

'Waiting for someone?' he asked.

'Oh, yes. A friend of mine is arriving from America,' I said nonchalantly.

While Ramsey and I were making small talk he said, 'Is that your friend — behind you?'

I spun around, and Laura was standing there smiling. Her long hair was tucked under a large straw hat and she was wearing a thick, warm jacket.

A few seconds earlier she had walked straight past me and I had not recognized her.

Sheepishly I apologized and then took her bags, and we set out on the drive to Beaurepaire House.

When we arrived at the old manor I could see Laura was impressed. 'You know', she said, 'I had conjured up ideas of what England would be like, and Beaurepaire House seems to embody them all.'

After I had shown her around we set off for a long walk in the woods with Bruno and Celia, and this time I left my shotgun in the closet. We talked about many subjects, and I promised to take her shopping and sightseeing in London the next day.

But the most important thing about those first few hours we were together was that we felt comfortable and at ease in each other's company.

When we arrived back at the house James had returned from his round of golf at Sunningdale. He had not seen Laura since the flight between Detroit and New York, and when I introduced Laura and Lois I was delighted to see there was instant rapport. There were lots of laughs as the four of us sat around the dinner table late into the night.

James told Laura how I had pestered him during the final round of the Open just the day before to check on her flight from the United States and make certain we had the arrival time accurately.

Next day Laura and I drove around London taking in all the traditional sight-seeing attractions the great city has to offer — St Paul's Cathedral, the Tower of London, the Houses of Parliament, Madame Tussaud's — and of course the great Oxford Street emporia.

Two years earlier, when I had won my first Martini International, BBC television had produced a twenty-minute special based on my quick success in England and my hopes and plans for the future.

The show was produced by John Phillips, with whom I became very friendly, and I was anxious for Laura to meet him. That night the three of us ate together at a restaurant in London's West End, and it proved to be a very expensive night out: when I got back to my car I was appalled to see that its gleaming red duco had been badly damaged by vandals, and the bill for restoring it came to £1,000 ($2,000).

After four wonderfully happy days Laura flew back home to America and

With Isao Aoki during the 1979 British Open at Royal Lytham and St Anne's.

83

James and I sat down to discuss the previous week's Open championship.

As I had planned many weeks before, I went to Royal Lytham and St Anne's well before the tournament started, determined to familiarize myself with the course. I needed to solve its mysteries, and develop in my mind the right sort of plan to play it.

Lytham really does provide an examination of a vastly different sort to most of the other famous British links courses. Most of Britain's seaside links are as nature made them, but there is ample evidence of the hand of man at work at Lytham, where shrubs, brushwood and man-made mounds give the course a different flavour. It is also one where the balance of holes is at variance with the ideals of present-day architects. Three of the four short holes come on the front nine holes, and two of the three par-fives are also met in the opening half.

It is a strange mix, where extraordinary sub-par bursts are almost common-place on the front half, but where the back nine can (and usually do) provide a cruel counter-balance.

Several of the par fours on the home half of the course were unreachable for most of the players in the field, and only the really long hitters had a chance of making them.

By the time the tournament started I felt I had done my homework well.

For the entire four days of the tournament the wind blew strongly from the north-west and it was bitterly cold. They were two-sweater conditions at the minimum, but I did notice several players add another one for good measure.

With Jack Nicklaus, Lee Trevino, Hale Irwin, Gary Player, Seve Ballesteros, Tom Watson and the Japanese with the freakish putting stroke, Isao Aoki, in the field, I had absolutely no illusions about the task ahead.

I finally finished in eighth place, and left Lytham with a twinge of disappointment because I had been in the firing-line with a round to go. My first three rounds were 73, 71, 72, which stood me at 3 over par and only five shots behind the leader, Hale Irwin, who shot two wonderful 68s and then followed them with a 75.

It was the mercurial Spaniard Seve Ballesteros who was finally to march away with the championship, and in doing so he became the youngest winner of the old title since young Tom Morris back in 1872. The foundation stone of his victory was a 65 in the second round that prompted Hale Irwin to quip, 'He must have left out a couple of holes.' In fact Ballesteros had played the fearsome final five holes in 4 under par — a miraculous run in the conditions. When, like Irwin, Ballesteros returned a third round of 75 they had come back to us all and set the stage for a great struggle over the final 18 holes. With a round to play Irwin was on 211, Ballesteros on 213, Nicklaus on 214, so I believed I was in with a chance if the breaks went my way in the final round.

There was no point in going on the defensive, but the final day did not treat me kindly, and I fell away to a 76.

I was a few groups ahead of Ballesteros, but the roars from the huge gallery around him gave every other competitor the unmistakable message that the Spaniard was having his adventures. In his final round of 70 he sparred many times with the rough, and at the 16th drove his ball into the car-park. But in the final analysis Ballesteros was the only player to break par — even if it was by just one shot — and he had a three-shot margin from Jack Nicklaus and Ben Crenshaw at the finish.

Although my final round was a disappointment, I would be remiss if I did not mention the great showing of my colourful countryman Roger Davis. Roger not only bedazzled the galleries with his eye-catching plus-twos and brightly coloured sweaters but at one stage actually led the tournament. He finished in fifth place, passing the stumbling Hale Irwin on the way up the order.

I sometimes think I am inclined to treat myself harshly in tournament post-mortems. Although I was disappointed at my final round, my eighth placing was by far the best I have achieved in the Open. I had only played there twice before, failing to qualify in my first attempt at Turnberry in 1977 and scoring a reasonably satisfactory 291 at St Andrews the year after, where Nicklaus scored his great triumph.

I still have not made up my mind whether my approach to the major titles of the world is the right one.

At Lytham in 1979, and again at Muirfield the following year, I took off the week before the Open to practise and get to know these great tests as thoroughly as I could before play started.

I am now coming around to the idea that it might be better to play the tournament the week before the major championship, and just 'let it come'.

With hindsight, my preparation for the Muirfield Open was wrong. I really made a tactical error that I can appreciate now and will certainly guard against in the future. I went to Muirfield the week before the Open started, and peaked both my golf game and my mental keenness far too early. I practised over the course and honed every shot in my bag with long sessions on the practice fairway, and four days before the title started I was ready.

And that was the whole trouble. By the time Thursday's first round came along I had already 'played' my tournament, and I scored accordingly. Four days earlier I had been like a dog on a leash. I had reached a high, and could not wait for the tournament to start.

When I walked onto the first tee I felt drained. I tried hard, but so many bad shots flew from my clubs, and so many chances were missed on the greens, that I was never in contention. I had been wound up far too early, and I paid the penalty.

Now if I take the week off before one of the majors I make certain that my practice schedule is paced, and not as frantic as the routine I set myself in 1980. So far the Open has not proved the happiest of tournaments for me, but to win it still remains my biggest ambition in golf. I will not be satisfied until I have.

Most of my success outside Australia has been in England and Europe, and when the Open comes around each year the pressures mount. The British Press is constantly searching the ranks of European players for someone who can repel the annual invasion from the other side of the Atlantic. Ballesteros was the first non-American to win the crown since South Africa's Gary Player was successful in 1974, and I am always linked with them in Press speculation as a player who can possibly win. I am delighted to know the Press think I can.

I cherish very strongly the wonderful relationship I enjoy with the British golf-writing fraternity. Ever since I first came to the country in 1977 they have been more than kind to me, and I believe firmly that as a body their knowledge of the game is unsurpassed. Their prophecies of a victory for Norman in the Open will hopefully one day come true.

It is always around Open time that my friends in both Australia and England

Heavy going: 1981 British Open.

write to wish me luck or telephone their good wishes. James Marshall even seems a little more on edge than usual as the Open gets closer, and when all these factors are combined the pressure slowly mounts.

As this is one of the great golf festivals of the world, the preliminaries take on a far greater significance than in any other tournament we play.

These additional pressures, the hopes and prayers of the people closest to me, must be carried through the Open week successfully if I am ever to win the oldest title of them all. Every year every competitor in the Open shares the same burden, and it is the men of true grit and character who emerge victorious, despite the extra psychological loads they shoulder.

When I was very young in golf my father Mervyn once walked off the course
in disgust as I displayed my anger in a flurry of club-throwing during a quite
unimportant club game at Virginia. In my youth I found giving an errant club
the good old heave-ho down the fairway a splendidly satisfying method of
letting off steam.

The day my father stopped following me at Virginia he left the club without
saying a word, but when I arrived home in the evening he sat me down in his
study and admonished me in terms that were unmistakable.

As a young man my father was an above-average rugby footballer and played
representative football in North Queensland as a second-row forward. He
rejected several offers to go south to Brisbane and play, preferring to pursue his
career, which has now taken him to a senior executive job with Mt Isa Mines
Holdings. He is currently the general manager (engineering services) for the
company, and in control of the development of a gigantic new coal-mining
enterprise in Queensland involving the building of a town, railway and a port as
well as other engineering developments.

There was a wealth of wisdom and experience behind what he had to say.

When my father walked away from me at Virginia on this particular day I had just sent my 7 iron cartwheeling down the fairway with my anger its main propelling force. Club-throwing seemed to me a perfectly natural way to release one's ire.

But I did not stop to think how it looked to outsiders. My father told me, 'If you ever throw a club again I will walk away from you. Son, I do not believe in that sort of thing. No self-respecting golfer or future professional would think of doing what you did today.'

My father's words sank in. I doubt if I have been guilty of throwing a club since, but there is no question that this game of golf can tear at your nerve-ends.

Certainly I have a temper. Sometimes I think I graduated with Straight 'A's' in this department, but over the years I have learned to keep it in check. When I look around me there are very few people who play top-level sport who can really bottle up their inner emotions. Take Lee Trevino. He is a nervous type of character, but when things go awry for Lee his comic act is his safety valve. Bjorn Borg did not let a thing upset him, but how different is John McEnroe? Even Jack Nicklaus has those glowering moments when the club is returned to the bag with a force that could send it through the bottom and disgust is written all over his face.

There is a fine line between temper and temperament, and being in control of both these ingredients is an essential prerequisite for success. I am at my angriest on a golf-course when I hit a bad shot, because I do not expect to hit bad shots. They upset me. As I am now aware, when I was a kid it got out of control, and I would follow one bad hole with another.

Now I am looking for a birdie, and expect to get it immediately after I have blundered. I can forget my bad shots a lot more quickly.

Sometimes I wonder if golf fans are genuinely aware of the pressures that go hand in hand with golf at international level. I find there is a tendency for them to invade the privacy of the players at the most inopportune times. When I go to the practice fairway before a round of golf I am going to my 'office' where I want to work and concentrate — to sort out any problems that I might have in my swing. That hour or so before the starter calls me to the tee is vitally important, and not the time for answering questions or signing autographs.

To draw a parallel, I can imagine the sort of reception I would get if I walked unannounced into a doctor's surgery and started asking questions, or went uninvited to the cockpit of a Jumbo aircraft and asked the captain for his autograph.

I know other players share my view on this subject.

It was in my fourth attempt to win the British Open that my temperament came under fire from the Australian Press.

Or was it my temper?

In the relatively short time I have been playing professional golf I think I have established a good winning record, but there is a gap in it that badly needs to be filled.

I need to win one of the world's major titles.

I have said elsewhere that I did not like the sort of golf test Royal St George's presented, but now I must qualify that statement by saying that the problem lies more with me. It is immaterial whether or not I like the course. I must find the

Opposite
A moment's relaxation with Arnold Palmer: 1981 British Open.

91

key that unlocks Britain's seaside links and admits my golf game, because these are the courses over which I will be examined for years to come.

Once again I peaked too early at Sandwich, and even Laura told me I was ready to play two days before the title started.

'He was pacing up and down waiting for the gun to go off. I tried to tell him in a subtle way to slow down because it wasn't a race,' Laura told one golf-writer.

I was well up after an opening round of 72, but my second round of 75 was a shocker, and put me right out of the tournament. I was in no mood to speak to anyone, and I am afraid the Press guys who wanted to talk to me immediately after the round discovered my other side.

One report back in Australia claimed :

> Greg Norman fell by the wayside with the second round 75 and put on a display of petulance that would have done John McEnroe proud. More seriously, for the future of Norman's golf, boiling temperament off the course spilled on to it the next day. Making a charge back into contention he misjudged a drive that wound up in a fairway bunker.
>
> Cursing as he strode after it Norman slashed at the sand all too hurriedly and had a bogey. He could not curb the tide of self destruction and picked up more bogeys on three of the next four holes. It was a crucial time in the world's premier Open tournament and Norman blew it ...

It is sobering indeed to see one's anger mirrored in the columns of a newspaper, and I readily admit my guilt. Those couple of days at Royal St George's were almost a throwback to my youth.

But I want my father to know I did not throw a club.

CHAPTER 13
A TOUCH LONGER?

I was tying up the laces on my golf-shoes when Seve Ballesteros walked past me in the locker-room at Wentworth Golf Club. In a few minutes' time I would head for the practice fairway and warm up for my quarter-final match against the Englishman Nick Faldo in the World Match Play championship.

It was 1980, and the year is important.

As Seve walked by he said, 'Good luck today.' Startled, I turned my head towards him and shot back, 'Good luck to you too.' The exchange is significant, because it was the first time in the years we had been playing the same tournament trail that we had spoken to each other, and it caught me by surprise.

Although I now count Seve as a good friend — and I believe he feels the same way about me — for years he was an enigma. Week after week we would see each other at tournaments, and we would walk right past each other without so much as a nod of the head. Even when we were drawn to play together, those rounds of golf were played without us exchanging a word.

Because golf is such a personal game it is understandable that each individual competitor protects and promotes his own image. His image is part of his livelihood.

To his public Seve is an outgoing young man with a wide, flashing smile. To the players around him it was a different story. He had arrived on the European scene a year before me, and I acknowledge that his tournament record is more impressive than mine. He has won two U.S. Masters and a British Open, and nobody admires his ability more than I do. But there is another side to the swashbuckling young man from the Spanish village of Pedrena that not only baffled me but also perplexed his compatriots on the European tour. Often I would ask them, 'What is wrong with Seve? Why does he carry on like this?' And they would shrug their shoulders and say, 'That's the way he is.'

In any sport rivalry is a healthy component, but when it reaches the stage of jealousy it has been carried an unhealthy step too far. Because I had won the Martini tournament at only my second appearance in England four years earlier I am convinced that Seve decided he would treat me to his own version of the famous 'Hogan Stare'.

I belive I am a reasonably gregarious character, far happier to make friends than not. But if Seve Ballesteros wanted to play it that way, then there was nothing I could do but accommodate him. During this 'ice age' between us I had

I look forward to playing
many rounds of golf with
Seve Ballesteros in the
future.

no doubt that he was practising a type of long-term gamesmanship on me, but I refused to let it affect my golf game. He obviously recognized me as a threat to the supremacy he had established in Europe, and that I was hell-bent on knocking him off his throne. Of course I was — and still am — but at least our rivalry is conducted in a much friendlier atmosphere than it was during those strange years.

Most of the players who compete regularly on the European circuit believe they can pinpoint the change in Seve's attitude. It came when he returned to Europe after his remarkable victory at Augusta in April 1980. He had proved a point, proved he was the King, and could now afford to be more expansive. Just as Walter Hagen said he could now find the time to 'stop and smell the flowers'.

When Seve's troubles with the European Tournament Players Division erupted over the appearance-money issue in 1981 he might have been surprised to learn that I was one of his strongest supporters. The demands he was making through his manager Ed Barner were in my opinion quite reasonable, because of the enormous boost he had given European golf. Although I was never publicly quoted in support of his stand, I argued strongly with officials of the ETPD that the healthy position of the European professional tour was due in no small way to the magnetism of the Spaniard. If sponsors were prepared to pay sums like $30,000 to import 'name players' like Tom Kite, Andy North and Fuzzy Zoeller into Europe, then Seve Ballesteros was worth more money than any of them. Only Jack Nicklaus would rate higher.

To me Ballesteros was worth the $24,000 a tournament he was reportedly asking because his record was far better than those of the well-paid imports. However, there was an undercurrent of resentment among the members of the ETPD which eventually forced Seve onto the tournament sidelines. Instead of displaying resentment they should have toasted Seve. In my opinion Ballesteros is the Arnold Palmer of European golf. In the same way that Palmer's enormous public appeal generated the popularity explosion of the game in America twenty odd years ago, the dashing Spaniard has captivated Europe.

When he eventually settled his differences in Europe Seve jumped back into tournament golf with all his old flair, winning the World Match Play title, the Scandinavian Open and the Australian PGA championship. He made a great many people swallow their words after his sensational return to the game, but by the same token I believe that Seve is a more mature and wiser man for the experience he went through. He is a far better and more perceptive person for it.

He is also a far more dedicated player than he was, and that attitude is an ominous sign for us all. Sometimes I believe he is a little too serious out on the course, but then I have never believed a golf-course is the place to do cartwheels anyway.

Close observers of the global golf arena are confidently predicting that Seve and I will battle for the major plums of the world tour over the next decade. I hope they are correct, and that a fair share of them come my way. I have watched him play a lot of golf, and it is a brave man who will point to a weakness in his game. If there was one, then it was in his driving, when he tried to cut down his length and manipulate the ball, but all that did was send him into a minor slump. Now he is back to his old cavalier rip from the tee, and that is helping him win tournaments again.

I have often been asked how we compare from the tee, each with our drivers out and each catching it flush. I have been described as the straightest long driver in the world, but when Seve and I each 'nail' one, then I believe he would get it past me.

He might say exactly the opposite. It is an academic question that proves nothing, but for the record they are my opinions.

The vast number of golf fans who make up the galleries, particularly in Britain, were probably unaware of Seve's aloofness towards his contemporaries.

It is a much happier atmosphere these days. The brick wall that existed between us started to crack after that small incident in the locker-room at Wentworth, and finally disappeared when our respective managers Ed Barner and James Marshall negotiated an exhibition series with Seve and me playing the South African lass Sally Little and Nancy Lopez-Melton. The matches were sponsored by the Phoenix insurance company, and played at the delightful Woburn Golf Club. We beat the girls 4-2, and I won $35,000 for my three days' work. The series was a mixture of stroke play, match play and Canadian foursomes, and it was here that Seve and I really enjoyed ourselves.

In this type of golf we both drive and then select the ball we want to play, so were able to stand up there and let fly, confident that one of us would be in a good position. I guess it was in these two-man duels from the tee that I gauged that Seve was a touch longer than I was.

For several days Seve and I played together, relaxed together and ate together as we got to know each other.

I enjoyed it, and I hope he did.

I look forward to playing many rounds of golf with him in the future.

CHAPTER 14
A HOLE TOO FAR?

With that Ballesteros reverie behind me, let us return to the World Match Play championship, where, you will recall, Englishman Nick Faldo was waiting for me on the frst tee for our second-round encounter. I was one of four fortunate players to be seeded in the tournament, along with America's Bill Rogers, Ballesteros and Japan's Isao Aoki, and with the luxury of a first-round bye we all enjoyed a day off waiting to see who would emerge from the first round, and just who our quarter-final opponents would be.

The concept of the World Match Play title is a good one because it gives the golf public the chance to see the top professionals in head-to-head contests — rare in these days of 72-hole stroke-play tests.

Match-play is the oldest form of golf, but it has been virtually pushed out of the professional arena altogether, with the lone exception of this event. Practically all the major national amateur championships are decided by match-play, and it does seem a pity that this is the only professional tournament to survive in this form. Once again the dictates of television are probably paramount in the demise of professional match-play tournaments, and it is simple to understand why. How ridiculous it would be for matches to finish on the 12th or 13th green when all the television crews are geared up for much later action! At least in stroke-play golf the television networks know that every player in the field must complete a full round of golf, and the crews are placed accordingly.

Personally, I enjoy the parry and thrust of match-play, the man-against-man encounters, because like most young Australian players I was brought up on that type of golf. Our inter-state series, our national championships, state championships and club championships, are all decided by this method, but once I left the amateur ranks behind me I also left behind the pleasures of match-play golf.

The match on which my attention was closely focused on that first day at Wentworth in 1980 was between my countryman David Graham and Faldo, because the winner of that contest was to be my opponent the next day.

I dare say that if I had been given the choice of playing either one of them it would have been Faldo, because I have a great regard for Graham's ability and tenacity. He can be a fearsome opponent, and apart from his skill on the golf course I consider him a close friend. He has often gone out of his way to offer me

Consulting the rule book: 1980 Suntory World Match Play Championship at Wentworth, England.

guidance and encouragement, and meeting him head-on was not a situation I would relish.

So I was absolutely astonished at the manner in which Faldo brushed Graham aside, a past winner of the championship and a winner also of the United States PGA crown. His wonderful victory in the U.S. Open was still a year away, but I firmly believed the machine-like golf for which he is renowned would prove too much for the Englishman.

In a huge upset Faldo was in control for most of the day, and finally sent my Australian friend back to the clubhouse 7-6. Faldo is an enigma on the European scene, and I think I use the word in its proper context. He is a young man of undoubted ability, and has been ahead of me in the pay-day queue on many occasions, although on balance I dare say I have headed the same queue more frequently than he has.

98

The most astute of Europe's golf-watchers remain perplexed by Faldo's failure to reach a level of consistency in his tournament golf, but on a given day he can be outstanding. Two victories in the British PGA title are good indicators of how well he can play.

When Marshall and I were discussing prospects on the morning of my match with Faldo I said to him, 'If Nick plays as well against me as he did against David, then it is going to be a tough day's work.' He agreed.

With hindsight I now realize just how fortunate I was to sneak past Faldo and make it into the semi-finals.

At lunchtime I was four down, and then six down after 25 holes, and I doubt if my most optimistic supporters would have risked a counterfeit pound-note on my chances of winning. I certainly would not have.

I was scheduled to return to Australia immediately the championships finished to fulfil a tournament commitment on the Queensland Gold Coast, and while we were walking to the 26th tee I thought I would be back home much earlier than I really wanted to be.

It is hard to pinpoint where the swing in my favour began, but as I walked to the tee I said to my caddie Scotty Gilmour, 'It is a matter of going for it now. We've got to take some chances.'

I won the 27th to put a slight dent in Faldo's big lead, and then the short 28th, where Nick dumped his tee-shot into the trees and an unfortunate spectator unwittingly came to my aid.

My ball hit him on the head and bounced back onto the green. I went on to win the hole, but only after I had checked on the spectator's condition. There was quite a deal of blood around and the man was obviously shaken up, but when I spoke to him he assured me that he was not seriously injured, and then wished me good luck.

After winning those two quick holes I maintained my momentum and whittled Faldo's lead away rather quickly, so that by the time we reached the 36th tee I was trailing by only one hole. The odds were still heavily in Faldo's favour, as he needed only a half to take out the match.

But now the pressure was right on him, as a match that had appeared dead just a few holes earlier had suddenly sprung to life again. While I had been languishing at six down most of the big gallery who had set out with us on that wet, cold day had wandered away in search of a contest with a little more excitement attached to it. They were back with reinforcements by the time we reached the last hole, as news of my comeback had spread quickly around the famous Burma Road.

The second round, or quarter-final matches, were played in foul conditions. It was cold and rainy and a strong wind blew all day, while it was the effect of the rain which ironically helped my cause.

When I teed up at the home hole — a long dog-leg par five — I firmly believed that my only chance of taking the match into overtime was to make a birdie. As it turned out I didn't — but the match did go extra holes. My second shot found a greenside bunker, and Faldo also missed the green. He pitched in to about eight feet, while my bunker shot finished fifteen feet away and it was my putt first. I missed.

So all Faldo had to do to beat me and go into the semi-finals was get down in two putts from eight feet, and that looked quite a simple task. I mentally resigned myself to my fate, and just waited for Nick to go through the formalities.

The putting surface was saturated. For most of the match we had been using squeegee boards to dry out the path to the hole, and as he prepared himself for the *coup-de-grâce* Faldo again asked for a squeegee. He carefully ran it the distance between his ball and the hole, and then carried it on several feet past the hole.

It was to prove a fatal mistake.

The squeegees flatten the grain of the grass going down the line of the putt, and conversely make any return putt into the grain that much more difficult.

Whenever I use a squeegee I always make certain that I dry out the area to the hole, but go no farther, because the water will halt the ball quickly if the putt is missed. I watched Faldo carefully, and I knew that if his putt was off line it would carry on a good distance past the hole going down-grain.

That is exactly what happened. His ball went almost five feet by and then 'jagged' coming back against the grain and he had three-putted from just eight feet. I won the hole with a five to square the match.

It was an unbelievable let-off.

Every umbrella in the huge crowd around the last green dipped in dismay, like flags going to half-mast, as Faldo stood there mortified. He could hardly believe what he had done, and neither could the gallery. Later I was to read one account of that dramatic 18th hole which said 'Faldo was so chagrined as to be beside himself for his dereliction on the 36th green ....'

I dare say I would have been too, if it had happened to me.

To suit the demands of television the 'overtime' holes started at the 15th, and as we headed into them darkness was close at hand and it was still raining. We halved the first extra hole, and we needed car headlights along the fairway to help us down the next. That hole is a relatively easy par 4, and I slipped a 9 iron onto the green eight feet away and holed it for a birdie and the match.

As we drove back to the clubhouse I glanced across and saw Nick walking alone in the half-dark. There were no words in the English language that could console him in that moment of despair. His closest friends wisely kept their distance as time started its slow healing process.

That evening I told Laura I felt like Houdini, and with the sort of luck I had had against Faldo I should go on and win the tournament.

In the first-round matches the day before there had been several surprises, with the young American Peter Jacobsen eliminating South African Gary Player 2-1, and prompting Gary to say, 'It is embarrassing to play like that. I couldn't even hit the fairway.'

The Scot Bernard Gallacher downed Japan's Haruo Yasuda and Sandy Lyle trounced George Burns 6-5.

The defeats of both Gary Player and David Graham were the real first-round upsets, but there were two more in store that rain-swept second day as Jacobsen was never behind in beating Ballesteros 3-2, and Gallacher forgot all about Bill Rogers's reputation to come from three down with nine holes to play and win on the last green. Rogers came to the tournament as the defending champion.

Gallacher was in my half of the draw, with Lyle and Jacobsen meeting in the other semi-final.

The second round had been completed despite dreadful weather conditions,

but it was impossible to play on the Saturday, so the semi-finals were put back a day with the final, then rescheduled for Monday.

Victory over Sandy Lyle at the final hole of the 1980 Suntory World Match Play Championship.

The timetable I was thinking about altering halfway through my match with Faldo was under scrutiny again, but this time for a different reason. It was now going to be a tight squeeze to get back to Australia in time for my appointment on the Queensland Gold Coast. When Sandy Lyle defeated Jacobsen 6-5, and I registered the same winning margin over Gallacher in the semi-finals, I could not have been happier.

I had a personal score to settle with Lyle. He is a good friend of mine, but earlier in the year he had stolen the top place in the European Order of Merit from me by just over $500 (£278).

A back injury had forced me to miss one tournament as the European season drew to a close, and when just one shot separated us in the Dunlop Masters it was enough for Sandy to tip me out of top place.

Lyle is a true Scot with plenty of guts and ability, well underlined by the way he had topped the European Order of Merit in successive years. Only good players can do that, so I had no illusions about the task I had ahead of me in the final.

Sandy is about as long as I am off the tee, but I went into the match believing I held a slight edge, mainly because of the greater accuracy in my long game.

Sometimes he will leave his wooden clubs in the bag and use a 1 iron, and around a course like Wentworth that can be a disadvantage.

The whole final really boiled down to the Burma Road's 502 yards dog-leg 18th hole. In a day of seesawing fortunes I went to lunch leading by just two holes, and when I still held that margin going to the 33rd I felt confident of success. Just four holes to go to claim a world title. Alongside me my caddie Scotty Gilmour whispered encouragement: 'Keep your head. You can win if you keep your head, but you still have plenty of golf to play.'

The moment I scented victory was the moment I let my guard down, and like a well-trained prize-fighter Lyle moved in with two damaging blows.

I three-putted and lost the 33rd; and two holes later I stood and watched Sandy down a courageous ten-footer to square the match. The roar from the crowd was deafening. The two-hole cushion I had enjoyed was gone.

And only the last hole to play.

Laura had taken three months' leave from her job in America to fly to England and watch me play the championship. We were then going to Australia together. I like to have her around when I am playing, to know she is in the gallery, and no matter how big the crowd I can always find her. We were booked to fly out of Heathrow that night, and as I walked to the final tee I thought how much happier the trip home would be if I could win the last hole.

The right-turn dog-leg at Wentworth's home hole is well guarded, and I knew that Sandy had a problem as he stood with his caddie pondering what club to play. Should he go with his driver or sacrifice vital distance with his 1 iron?

Like me, he was desperate for a birdie, and the driver was the only club that could set it up for him. He took it out of his bag slowly, carefully lined up his shot, and then pushed it wide into the tree-line to the right. It was well off the target line to the hole, and tucked awkwardly behind the dog-leg. He could not make the green in two shots.

My drive went straight down the left side of the fairway, well away from the dog-leg and its attendant problems, and finished in the light (and well-trampled) rough with still about 250 yards to go to the green. That is a little farther than I normally reckon on hitting my 3 wood, but I had enough adrenalin stored up to hit it a mile.

Sandy was away first and punched his ball into the middle of the fairway but still well short of the green, and only a miraculous third shot could get him close enough for a birdie.

While Scotty and I were standing there gazing at the distant green I had already made up my mind what club to hit, and then I turned to Scotty for confirmation. He already had the 3 wood out of the bag with the head cover removed. 'Give it everything,' he said.

'Settle down ... don't rush it ... back slowly ...' all these factors went through my mind as I moved in over the ball, and the result could not have been better.

The ball went like an arrow to the heart of the green, and finished twenty feet

from the hole. I lagged up close by the hole, and when Sandy missed he conceded my birdie putt for the championship. I stood there for several seconds savouring the moment and letting those four words roll through my brain ... 'World Match Play Champion ...', and then I searched the crowd for the one person with whom I wanted to share that moment — Laura. 'Wonderful, wonderful,' repeated Laura.

Immediately the presentation ceremony was completed Laura and I sped to Heathrow airport with our twelve pieces of luggage for the flight to Australia. In my pocket was a cheque for £30,000 ($60,000), by far the largest single prize I had ever won.

Once we had settled into our seats Laura and I sipped a glass of champagne each, and then I fell asleep. It was my only concession to a celebration. I was absolutely drained.

The year 1980 had been good to me. Apart from my World Match Play title, I had won the Scandinavian and the French Open at St Cloud by a record margin of ten shots.

Both these wins were against the best fields in Europe, and when I shot rounds of 67, 66, 68, 67 in the French championship I played a brand of golf for four days that would have been difficult to surpass. My score was 20 under par.

The Scandinavian Open victory I also look back on with considerable satisfaction because it was achieved despite a lamentable first round of 76 which left me trailing the leader, my countryman Graham Marsh, by eight shots. But my next three rounds of 66, 70, 64 made up all that lost ground until I finally won the title by three shots from Mark James, with Seve Ballesteros, Sandy Lyle and Bob Charles in a tie for third place. My final round was a course record, and my total of 276 a handsome 12 under par.

There was one significant factor midway through the European season of 1980 which also exerted a big influence on my performances, and that was the chance hiring of a ruddy-faced, stockily built Scotsman as my caddie.

I met 'Scotty' Gilmour a few days before the Irish Open at Portmarnock when my regular caddie on the European tour arrived at the club the worse for drink, leaving me no alternative but to dismiss him on the spot. He was not capable of walking around the course, let alone carrying a fully laden golf bag over his shoulder as well.

The caddies in Great Britain are a colourful collection of characters, and a vital part of the tournament scene. As a group they are usually reliable and trustworthy, and to a player a good caddie is worth his weight in gold. They gravitate to the golf-tour from a wide variety of backgrounds, and it is not uncommon to discover that many of them are well educated, and simply using golf as an alternative life-style. Of course, there is a hard core among them who have been caddieing for most of their lives, and it was from these that Scotty Gilmour came. He lived through the agonies and ecstasies of many tournaments alongside me, and a strong bond was formed between us.

Before he slung my bag across his shoulder Scotty had worked for a string of excellent players, including Tony Jacklin and Gary Player. He had also worked the United States golf-tour, and was once Tom Weiskopf's regular, so he came to me as a man with top credentials and a man who understood his trade thoroughly.

Initially our agreement was on a casual basis, but after Gilmour worked for me

for two or three tournaments I asked him if he would like the job permanently.

He said he would.

The day I hired him at Portmarnock I had arranged to partner Stewart Ginn against Sam Torrance and John O'Leary in a match where the side bets were high.

After the middle of 1980 Gilmour worked alongside me all over the world and together we won six tournaments, including the World Match Play championship and an Australian Open, but our partnership ended in 1982 when I went to Canada and America to compete in the Canadian Open title and the American PGA championship. Scotty had assured me he would be there for both tournaments, and when he had not arrived by the eve of the Canadian Open I started to worry. When he did not appear the next day for the first round not only did I have to find another caddie but I was starting to feel very angry with Scotty. I had not heard from him, and had no idea of his whereabouts.

The following week the tour moved south to Tulsa, Oklahoma, for the PGA title, the last of the 1982 majors, and I was desperately keen to win the tournament — along with a whole lot of other guys.

Still no word from Scotty, and again I had to find another caddie, but I had also made up my mind that when I returned to England I would be asking for a 'Please explain' from Scotty Gilmour.

Ray Floyd, the onetime playboy of American golf, emerged as the winner of the PGA title after four boiling hot days under the Oklahoma sun, laying the

Facing the press after winning the 1980 Suntory World Match Play Championship.

105

The 1980 Suntory Match Play Champion nearly loses his trophy!

foundation for his second victory in the championship with a breathtaking opening round of 63. I was well satisfied with my opening 66 and a share of second place with Bob Gilder, and at the halfway mark I was only three shots behind Floyd.

On the last hole of both the third and fourth rounds I made bogeys, which eventually meant all the difference between running second and my ultimate share of fifth place.

I was playing alongside Ray on the last day, and by the time we came to the final hole I was aware that I needed a birdie to have any chance of running second. There was no chance of winning, as Floyd had long since shaken off his pursuers and could have taken an eight at the final hole and still won.

In fact he took six, to lead home Lanny Wadkins by three shots.

I elected to hit a 3 iron for my second shot into the final green, and the ball pitched just short of pin-high and then skipped off the back of the green, only

106

four or five feet from the cut surface but buried deep in the 'barbed-wire' grass at the back of the green.

My recovery shot saw the ball just escape from the long rough and reach the edge of the green, a good 25 feet from the hole. The putt hit the hole and stayed out, and the resultant bogey was very costly, pushing me out of a share of third place into a share of fifth place.

It was a disappointing finale, as for most of the tournament I was holding down second place, and on a couple of occasions had played myself into a position to threaten Floyd's grip on the championship.

By the eleventh hole of the last round I was only a couple of shots away from the leader when I spotted Ray walk over to the gallery ropes and exchange a few words with his little wife Maria. Whatever she said to him fired Ray up again, because it was almost a procession from there home as he recaptured the form that had given him such a commanding lead for most of the tournament.

There is little doubt that Ray Floyd's whole outlook on life changed after he met Maria back in 1973, when he enjoyed his playboy image far more than the dedication necessary to maintain his place in the golf world. He is now the model husband, with three young children, the 1976 U.S. Masters title and two American PGA championships alongside his name.

I met Scotty Gilmour in Dublin the following week for the Irish Open title at Portmarnock, and although he worked for me during that tournament I was not satisfied with his explanation for not arriving for both the Canadian Open and American PGA championships.

We parted company and my new caddie was a Londoner, Peter Coleman, who could play to a 4 handicap, and told me that he took up caddieing full-time when he divorced his wife several years ago.

Coleman stayed with me for several months, but early in 1983 I realized I was missing Scotty, and decided to give him another chance — if he wanted it. I rang him from Australia and told him I would forgive him, and asked him if he would like to try again.

'My oath, I would' came back the reply, so the old firm is back together again and all is forgiven.

CHAPTER 15
THE AUSTRALIAN OPEN

The Australian Open championship is a tournament that has sent me through the whole range of human emotions, and is a tournament that I might have won in three successive years.

But only once in those three years did I in fact enjoy the thrill of capturing the Open championship of my own country, and that success came in 1980, when I defeated fellow-Australian Brian Jones by a bare shot at The Lakes Golf Club in Sydney. It was the year before and the year after that win, 1979 and 1981, that really hurt me because on both occasions I felt I had the title in my keeping only to falter at the very last hole.

Every major golf tournament brings its share of heartache and hard-luck stories, just as every tournament brings joy to the man who ultimately triumphs. These ingredients are the very essence of championship golf, and there is not one successful player in the world who has not experienced the dismay at losing when he knows he should have won, or the thrill of winning when he is well aware that luck has run alongside him. In the three years I would like to review now I think that I had more of the negative ingredient on my side than I deserved, and certainly in 1979 Jack Newton had more than his fair share of the lucky breaks. By saying that I do not want the reader to interpret my remarks as sour grapes because that is exactly the impression I am trying to avoid, and I will try to substantiate my argument.

Jack Newton is to Australian golf of the modern era what Ossie Pickworth represented to the game twenty years or so ago: a character of enormous magnetism who treats the game with an outwardly casual approach, chain-smoking his way from tee to green, and when the day's work is finished always ready to slap a dollar on the bar and enjoy himself.

I did not know Pickworth, nor did I see him play, but I have read and heard enough about him to know that he would fit into the category where I place Jack Newton. Just as Pickworth must have done, Newton relies heavily on his natural ability and great fighting heart, because there is no doubt in my mind that these factors in his make-up earned him his one-shot win over myself and Graham Marsh in that drama-packed Australian Open of 1979 at Melbourne's great Metropolitan layout.

I am not a great admirer of Newton's life-style, because I firmly believe that

Opposite
Caddie Peter Coleman gives the ball a final polish. And I think I have picked the right line for the putt. Coleman came to Australia to work for me during the 1982 season.

108

the long-range penalties represent too great a risk, and can quickly turn a player's career down-hill. At the time of writing Newton has not won a tournament since his one-shot victory at Metropolitan back in 1979.

However, Jack Newton had no long-range interpretation of his future in mind in that November week of 1979 when, in a field packed with a wonderful gathering of international and local golfers, he set out to win the Australian Open — and did.

The reigning British Open champion, Seve Ballesteros, and the current holder of the United States PGA title, David Graham, were top of the bill, alongside the U.S. Masters champion Fuzzy Zoeller, in what was possibly the hottest field ever assembled for an Australian Open. Without Jack Nicklaus facing the starter that may appear an extravagant statement, but the Golden Bear (who had won the year before in Sydney) decided not to defend.

It was a decision based more on the political climate of Australian golf at the time. The year before, his friend Kerry Packer had ended his agreement with the Australian Golf Union, and with the end of that agreement the tournament was moved away from The Australian Golf Club in Sydney for the first time in four years. Backed by the Packer financial resources, Jack had remodelled The Australian's layout, and was keen for the Open to be played there.

It was the depth of that field in 1979 that gave the Australian Open championship its world-class appearance. Apart from the Ballesteros-Graham-Zoeller trio, the 1979 Open's all-star cast included seven times winner Gary Player, former U.S.Open Champion Hubert Green and two young Americans Scott Tuttle and Bill Britton, who were eventually to have a far greater influence on the tournament than any of the Superstars. Dunhill were the sponsors, and despite the relatively poor showing of their expensive imports their name value had the desired result, and Metropolitan's fairways were packed for each of the four days of the tournament.

As in many 72-hole tournaments, all the excitement was crammed into the final round, which I started with a one-stroke lead over the field after scoring 73, 69, 73 on the first three days. My golf had been consistent and solid, with Metropolitan's narrow fairways and treacherous greens surrendering birdies only grudgingly.

My total of 215 gave me the barest breathing-space from Newton, whose first three rounds of 74, 72, 70 were a reflection of the confidence he was about to take into the final round. Alongside Newton was the real surprise packet of the tournament, young American Scott Tuttle, who entered Oregon University on a basketball scholarship and left it as a golfer.

When Tuttle fired those first three rounds of 73, 72, 71 to give himself a share of second place alongside Newton he had upstaged so many of his more famous countrymen that even they were moved to ask, 'Who is he?'

Like Britton, he had come to Australia for experience. Neither player held a ticket for the U.S.tour, and when they finally shared fifth placing and picked up $5,700 each they had well and truly paid for the experience they were looking for.

I played the second round of the title alongside Fuzzy Zoeller and Hubert Green, and if the final result left me a disappointed man the round with the two Americans was great fun.

Green lured Fuzzy and myself into a long-hitting contest, and the crowd loved

110

it.'Which of you two guys can hit the ball the longest?' he said, and with the gallery urging us on Fuzzy and I let rip with a few drives that had them yelling. Both of us were always careful to make certain we did not take foolish risks, and as I finished with 69 and the tournament lead no harm was done.

I outdistanced him more often than he outhit me, but with a round to play six shots covered the first sixteen players, and in that group I quickly recognized that the threats would come from Graham Marsh, Bob Shearer, the tenacious Gary Player ... and of course, Newton.

The first round had virtually wiped Ballesteros from contention, and after an opening 79 he just squeezed into the halfway cut with a second-round 73, while Hubert Green 76, and Ed Sneed 80, were never serious threats. And when David Graham opened with a pair of 74's, and Zoeller was one worse at the halfway mark, the main overseas challenge had virtually gone.

Newton had put the writing on the wall that his golf game was on the up with a nine-shot victory in the NSW Open shortly before the National title, and I came to Metropolitan with two victories for the year to my credit, the Hong Kong Open and the Martini International.

For both of us the Australian Open was vitally important. My parents had flown down from Brisbane to watch me play, and more than anything I wanted to win for their sake.

And Laura was there too, on her first visit to Australia.

If there are any two holes in the world that seem to have a hoodoo on my golf game, then they are the 9th and 10th holes at Metropolitan. I have played them many times now in major championships, and rarely have I parred them back-to-back in a tournament round. The hoodoo stuck with me during the final round of the Australian Open. Both holes are dog-legs, with the 439-yard 9th hole turning right into a particularly well-guarded and treacherous two-tiered green, while the 10th turns left with the driving position well guarded by a tree-line. During the final round of the 1979 Open I thought I might have laid a ghost to rest when my second shot was comfortably on the green at the 9th, but then I contrived to three-putt. I told myself that little damage had been done, as I was still through the halfway mark in 35, and when I heard that Newton had turned in 36 I was satisfied with my two-shot lead at that point. But how quickly situations change!

I double-bogeyed the next, when my second shot went through the green, and the six I took was to prove fatal. Ahead of me I heard the roar from Newton's gallery, and subsequently learned that he had holed out for a birdie from off the back of the green at the short 11th.

By the time I had played the same hole a few minutes later we were level pegging, and then Jack was in all sorts of bother at the long 14th where he finally curled home an eight-footer for a double bogey seven.

Once again I was back in front, but only by a shot, and when the gallery exploded into cheers ahead of me at the 15th I knew it was ominous. Jack had done it again. This time he had chipped into the hole for a birdie, and the wrestle for supremacy was on in earnest.

While Jack and I were playing our cat-and-mouse game a hole apart Bob Shearer was setting Metropolitan alight with a birdie surge that brought the big Victorian pro right into contention. The Shearer broadside started at the short 11th and went right on through the 15th, but that sort of superhuman pace could

not be maintained, and he finished with a bogey run that wiped out his challenge.

By the time I reached the 17th green in the final round I knew that Jack had finished with a level par round of 72 and an even par total of 288 for the tournament. I had hit my second shot into 7 feet at the 17th, and knew that a birdie on either of the last two holes would bring me in a shot under Newton and give me the championship.

The putt I was facing was uphill and moving slightly left to right — it was the sort of putt I enjoy most — and after reading it carefully I felt confident as I stood over the ball.

I struck it perfectly, but just a fraction too wide of the left lip, and watched in disbelief as the ball kissed the side of the hole and stayed out.

Now it was a birdie to win and a par to tie as I walked to the final tee. The 441-yard last hole is a straightaway affair with a two-tiered green, and for the Open the fairway was lined on both sides by brightly coloured entertainment and exhibitors tents. By now the scenario of the entire tournament was well known to the thousands of people inside those tents, and they spilled out to line the fairway ropes as I made my attempt to win, tie or lose this championship.

My drive split the fairway. I told myself as I walked through that crowded canyon of tents and humanity that my second shot must be on the top tier of the green, and when I struck my second shot that is exactly where the ball flew. My heart sank as I watched it slowly suck back down the slope onto the bottom tier, leaving me a putt of about twenty feet for the birdie I needed to be Australian Open champion. 'I must go for it,' I told myself. On reflection, perhaps, I should have played it safe, made sure of the par to tie and then gambled on beating Jack in a play-off. But I didn't.

My first putt dribbled four feet past the hole and now I was facing a real teaser to tie. Around the last green fifteen thousand pairs of eyes were glued on the drama unfolding, and on television millions more were holding their breath as I stepped up to the ball. 'Left lip and not too firm,' I told myself.

But as soon as I hit that little putt I knew it was too hard, and just as my birdie chance had behaved at the previous hole this putt did the same. It hit the top lip and spun out.

I have often been asked how I reacted at that moment, what went through my mind at the realization I had lost.

When I saw that little putt to tie swing off the lip my mind went black. My body froze. The combination of disappointment and disbelief were merged into a nightmarish experience that I will never forget. I still believe I should have won the tournament, because I believe I played some of the best golf of my life through those tough four days at Metropolitan.

There is an old saying in this game — 'Every shot in golf makes somebody happy.' As I tapped in the little putt for second spot with Graham Marsh I was conscious of the joy in the Newton camp. His mother and father were ecstatic. His wife Jackie was in tears, and a beaming Jack was surrounded by an army of excited, backslapping fans. High in the stands my mother Toini was also weeping, but for an opposite reason.

Although I had lost a tournament I believe I should have won, in a strange way the loss was a compensation for Newton that I understood. Four years earlier he had three-putted the last green at Carnoustie to let America's Tom

Opposite
The missed putt which cost me the 1979 Australian Open played at the Metropolitan, Melbourne.

113

Watson sneak into a tie with him in the British Open, and then he had lost the play-off next day by a shot as Watson shot 71 to Jack's 72.

In the second round of the British title Jack shot a wonderful 65, and he had those figures made up on a silver chain he wore around his neck on that final day at Metropolitan. His victory in 1979 went part of the way to laying to rest the ghost of Carnoustie, because everybody in the game is well aware just how much losing that championship cost Jack, and how much winning it meant to Watson. It is a cruel sport.

I would like to quote to you a couple of assessments of Jack's final round at Metropolitan.

Of his own golf Jack said, 'I played a load of rubbish. Houdini could not have got out of some of the spots I found myself in today.'

And Gary Player's observation was: 'Like Ballesteros in the British Open, he was all over the course. But he did not let it affect him and he kept playing like a winner. I take my hat off to him the way he kept fighting his way out of trouble.'

But the 1979 Open did not end for me when I had handed in my card.

After I had congratulated Jack I set off for the locker-room with my father, my caddie and a small group of friends to change my shoes and pack my bag. We were a disconsolate gathering as we talked quietly about the championship that had got away. While we were engaged in our post-mortem, unbeknown to me my name was being called to join the official party for the presentation ceremony about to begin beside the 18th green.

As joint runner-up with Graham Marsh that is where I should have been instead of in the locker-room. But nobody had told me the presentation ceremony was going to take place immediately my last group had holed out.

After I had done my packing my father and I wandered through the club's main corridor to the club lounge where my mother and Laura were waiting for us and everybody was feeling quite miserable. I told them to brighten up because what had happened out on the golf course a few minutes earlier was bound to happen again some day.

It is all part of playing professional golf for a living. One must learn to take the bitter with the sweet.

While we were sipping a drink I was appalled when a tournament official approached me and asked, 'Where were you? They have been calling for you at the presentation.'

On the way to the clubhouse shortly after I had holed out I had passed two Australian PGA officials (one being President Peter Thomson) on the way to the presentation area.

Not one official, not one representative of the sponsoring company, had taken the time to acquaint me with the presentation details, but when I was not there the inference to the public was unmistakable.

If anybody believes I missed that presentation ceremony because I was licking my wounds in disappointment they are totally incorrect. It was my duty to be there, and I should have been there. My absence could have been interpreted as a reflection on my sportsmanship, and I strongly resent that imputation.

Immediately I became aware of the situation I went to the tournament committee and blew my top. 'Why wasn't I told about the presentation?' I demanded. 'Nobody told me it was going on immediately.'

If the incident left a sour taste in anyone's mouth, that certainly included mine. The Australian PGA told the Press that I would be fined a 'nominal' amount for my non-attendance, but I have never heard from them. I am certain they realize the mistake was as much their fault as anybody's. I was so upset about the implications of my absence from the presentation ceremony and the conclusions that might be drawn from it that the next day I sat down and wrote a letter of explanation to the sponsors, the Australian Golf Union and the Australian PGA. I still have a copy.

Although I will never forget the anguish of Metropolitan in 1979, it was slowly moving into the recesses of my mind when I came back to Australia the following year to try once again to win the Australian Open.

I had put together a very successful European season with wins in the Scandinavian and French Opens, and just a few weeks earlier had won the World Match Play championship at Wentworth. It had been an exhausting year, but rewarding, and it would be even more so if I could cap it with the Australian title.

I believe I had every reason to feel confident because the tournament was being played over one of my favourite layouts at The Lakes Golf Club in Sydney, which I consider tailor-made for my target game. I had set the course record there with a 64 two years earlier, and in the lead-up practice rounds I was striking the ball strongly.

Laura had come to Australia with me again, and I was anxious for her to see the new house I had bought at Paradise Point, just north of Surfer's Paradise on the Queensland Gold Coast. It had a water frontage, and I had my new cruiser tied up at the jetty just across the lawn from the back door. I had named the house Divot, and the cruiser *Divot II*.

Together they had put a sizeable hole in my bank account, so I guess the names were appropriate.

It was an idyllic location, and for a few brief days we spent our time swimming in the pool or speeding across the calm waters aboard *Divot II*. We made plans to redecorate the house but never did complete them, because the secluded retreat I believed I had bought was suddenly discovered. Several times I answered knocks at the front door to find complete strangers standing there. When I inquired their business they asked, 'Are you Greg Norman?' And when I assured them I was they asked for my autograph. Hardly the ideal hideaway.

When Laura and I reached Sydney we scarcely discussed the tournament ahead. We both had our memories of the year before, and we both had our hopes and ambitions for 1980. There was no need to talk about it. I was disappointed that my mother Toini and my father Merv could not make the trip from Brisbane, but my mother had taken a tumble down the stairs at our home and sprained her ankle. But I know she did not move far from the television set for those four days.

The field at The Lakes was almost as impressive as it had been the year before at Metropolitan, with Seve Ballesteros trying again for a championship that keeps eluding him and David Graham back once again from the U.S. to demonstrate in a very tangible way his support for Australian golf. Certainly Graham is well compensated for his yearly excursions back to Australia, but the man has a real loyalty to golf there, and will never forget that it all started for him 'Down Under.'

Apart from these two Superstars, Hale Irwin, John Schroeder and that great

Scottish player Sam Torrance were in the field, and of course Jack Newton was back to defend the title he had nipped from under my nose the year before. Irwin, winner of two U.S. Open championships in 1974-79, was never really a threat after posting a second-round 77, but when I looked over the field the task looked no easier than it had appeared twelve months earlier. I was under no illusions.

I had returned to Australia on a 'high' after my successful European season, and although I played a couple of lead-up tournaments before going to Sydney it was the Open championship on which I had my sights set.

Victory this year would be no consolation for my loss at Metropolitan because there could be no consolation for what happened to me there. It was simply a case of a different venue — same tournament, get out there and win if you can.

Strangely I had a victory premonition after only six holes of the first round. I had picked up two early birdies, and felt at peace with the world. I felt I was coasting along in a rhythm that would take me to victory. I spoke to nobody about my premonition, not even Laura, and although there were many anxious moments it all came true in the end.

But there was one man who very nearly put paid to all this star-gazing, and it was the courageous little Brian Jones, unquestionably one of Australia's most underrated professional players.

There is not a lot of Brian Jones, the curly-haired Sydneysider who has lived and played in Japan for several years now but is always back in Australia for the spring and summer tours.

In the final outcome I guess I did to Brian what Jack Newton did to me just a year earlier. For most of the four days he was the pace-setter, building carefully on his opening 68 with rounds of 71 and 73 so that with a round to play he was 4 under par and two shots ahead of myself, with Billy Dunk lurking one shot adrift of me and David Graham on a level par total of 216.

I did not have to look too far down the list to see the name 'Ballesteros'. He was on 217 with a round to play, and a final charge could bring the Spaniard into the thick of the fight. But he went backwards instead, and with a quadruple bogey 8 at the 12th had a final round of 77. Poor Seve. I believe he caused a bit of chaos on the freeway that runs alongside the 12th fairway when he hooked his tee shot into the traffic.

Alongside me on 2 under par with a round to go was another young man, South Australian Roger Stephens. Open championships often throw up the rank outsider who hangs around for the first couple of days and then disappears into the ruck, but once Stephens had fired openers of 69-71 he just refused to go away.

Stephens worked as an assistant to Adelaide professional Brian Crafter, and left his pro-shop chores to play in Sydney. He eventually finished in fourth spot, and I was delighted when the Australian Golf Writers Association recognized his plucky display and sent him to Europe the following year. Crafter was part of the Australian Broadcasting Commission's television commentary team for the tournament, and there was a very understandable touch of pride in his voice when he talked about his young protégé. And Roger made sure that his 'Master' and the other commentators talked about him often by clinging on right to the finish.

I was drawn alongside David Graham during the final round, and we were in

the second last group to tee off. I was still two shots away from the lead, but I will never forget the opening nine holes of that last day when everything I touched turned to gold — well, almost. I birdied four of the first seven holes, including a hat-trick of them from the second, and reached the turn in 32. The way I had the ball running I felt I could have birdied the first eight holes in a row. It was a fantastic feeling. My burst swept me to the lead, but Brian Jones was not about to turn the last round into a 'lap of honour' for my sake. He was fighting like a cornered tiger, and picked up birdies at the 3rd and 5th holes before colliding with a bogey at the 7th. When he snaked in another birdie at the short 9th we both stood 6 under par with the watery back-nine ahead of us to decide the outcome.

Whenever Brian Jones looks back on the 1980 Open he will curse the closing holes at The Lakes because they were the holes where the mistakes he made were as critical to my winning chances as they were to his. He bogeyed the 15th, 16th and 17th in succession, and they were the blunders that finally turned the tide of fortune my way.

The tension over the final holes was incredible. Because I was playing in the group ahead of Jones I knew I had to set a score and force him to better it if he could. For me the crisis hole was the 16th, where I stood over a six-footer to save par — and the memories of Metropolitan's last hole the year before suddenly rushed into my mind.

The putt was longer than the one I missed a year earlier, but the message was the same. I broke my stance and went for a quiet little walk around the green to get it out of my mind. I holed it. In the final analysis that putt turned out to be the winning shot, because Jones came along and three-putted it for a bogey that dropped him a shot in arrears.

We both bogeyed the 17th and both parred the short 18th, but that simple statement of fact is far too flippant for the hour of drama contained in the playing of those two holes. When The Lakes is being attacked by its membership the 17th hole is a par 5 with a double water carry. The Australian Golf Union had reduced it to a par 4 for the Open, but whatever its rating it is a hole that requires a lot of thought and a very careful playing plan.

On this final day I elected to hit a 1 iron from the tee because I knew perfectly well that a driver-hit flush would only take my ball into the second water hazard — and that would be fatal. In fact my 1 iron kicked wickedly forward from a fairway pimple and finished perilously close to the hazard anyway.

I was faced with a shot of 220 yards to the flag. It had to be a 5 iron. I caught it on the sweet spot, and watched in horror as it pitched short of the green and then darted through, finishing well behind the putting surface. It was a clubbing error that could have proved disastrous. The club I should have hit was a 7 iron, and when I walked away with a bogey I cursed myself for the blunder.

The closing hole at The Lakes is 194 yards long and well guarded by traps. I took a 4 iron out of my bag and carved it into the right-hand bunker, still cursing myself over the blunder at the previous hole. The bunker shot I played was very forgettable, leaving me a 12-footer for par, but as soon as I hit that putt I knew it was in. I followed it across the green and gave a whoop, as it plopped into the centre of the hole. I walked into the scorer's caravan adjacent to the last hole and went through my card carefully, ticking off each hole as I went. By now I knew that Jones had also bogeyed the 17th, and needed a birdie on the last to tie. I could not get the 17th hole out of my mind.

Just as Jack Newton awaited his fate at Metropolitan the year before, I sweated it out in 1980. Through the window of the caravan I saw Jones's ball pitch on the green and run to the back about eight yards from the hole. It seemed an age before he finally got over it for that vital putt — a putt that would either send me into a play-off or see me hailed as the new Australian Open champion. When the ball was halfway to the hole I knew it did not have a chance.

If at Metropolitan the year before I had helped Jack Newton lay to rest the nightmare of Carnoustie, then Brian Jones had in turn helped me erase the Metropolitan memories that had haunted me for a year. The victory premonition I had on the very first day of the tournament had come true, but not before I had survived many agonizing moments.

For Jones it was another near miss. He had run third in this title to Gary Player in Perth several years earlier, and it was only in the last few holes that he surrendered his lead at The Lakes. For me the victory was a milestone. I had fulfilled an ambition I had held ever since the game of golf had wooed and won me as a teenager.

Writing in *The Australian* next day, Tom Ramsey said, 'There is no doubt Norman has the ability to become one of the world's greatest players. He has plenty of heart, a generous slice of nerve and oceans of confidence. He has these qualities in abundance plus that highly marketable quality — charisma', while in *The Melbourne Age* Peter Thomson was moved to write, 'The fates gave back to Norman what was whipped away from him last year at Metropolitan … .'

My victory at The Lakes shook a great weight off my back. Nobody can help reading newspapers, and although it is wonderfully flattering to read what other people think about my golf, if I had not won that battle out there with Brian Jones they would have thought I wasn't as good a player as they keep saying I am. The $35,000 I collected from the victory rounded off a year that had grossed me nearly a quarter of a million dollars. That victory also earned me an invitation to play the U.S. Masters the following April, and there is no price tag on that.

Laura and I flew back to Brisbane next day, and that night in my parents' home at Aspley — where it all started so long ago — we sat down for a small family celebration dinner. After that Laura and I headed south to Paradise Point, where for the next few weeks we fished and cruised on the Broadwater and I pushed golf out of my mind. I needed the break, I needed to recharge my batteries, because 1981 was going to be a big year.

Unquestionably one of the easiest and most pleasant tasks on the world golf-tour is to like Bill Rogers. If there is any golfer on the circuit who does not, then he is out of step with the majority, but in liking this charming, easy-going Texan one must not allow oneself to forget that when you tee-up against him you are teeing up against a mean competitor. I don't know why I should like the guy so much.

In 1980 I held The Australian Open, and a year later Bill Rogers had taken it away from me.

Victoria Golf Club's layout in the very heart of Melbourne's famous sand-belt country was the venue for the 1981 Australian Open, and I could not have been happier. It was a course I knew well, and the Australian Golf Union had set it up as befits a tournament of this standing, bringing the rough in tight and

The wedding party outside St Mary's Church, Springfield, Virginia on 1 July 1981. My mother and father are on the left. Laura's parents on the right.

minimizing the landing areas off the tee. When Bill Rogers arrived for the tournament he reckoned it was as narrow in places as Merion had been a few months earlier, when David Graham had written himself into the history books by becoming the first Australian ever to win the U.S. Open.

I came to Victoria as a married man. Laura had accepted my proposal of marriage earlier in the year as we drove away from The Masters at Augusta, and the date was set for 1 July in St Mary's church in Springfield, Virginia. It was a small but wonderful wedding. I had met Laura's parents — Jay, a senior company executive, and his wife Laura — and their two sons Richard and Jay jnr. a year earlier, and we had all got along well together. My parents Toini and Merv flew across from Australia for the ceremony.

But back to Victoria Golf Club.

Peter Thomson is considered the elder statesman of Australian professional golf as befits a man of his stature in the game. He was the first player from this country to win the British Open, and after his initial success in 1954 went on to capture four more. His great deeds are recorded for all time on a plaque in the main bar of the Victoria Golf Club, the club where we were playing the championship, and a club where Thomson started his golf and is an honorary member. Since he stepped away from the tournament scene he has become involved as a special golf commentator with the *Melbourne Age* newspaper, and is also on the Australian Broadcasting Commission's television golf team.

But it was as a newspaper critic that Thomson earned the ire of most of

Australia's top contenders for the Australian Open. Thomson declared that 'When the chips are down we have no one who can keep from hooking into trouble or three putting ... the trouble is that our professional squad loses the psychological fight before a shot is ever fired in anger ... .'

The four major events leading up to the Australian Open in 1981 had all been won by visiting overseas players — Ireland's Eamonn Darcy winning the CBA West Lakes Classic, Bill Rogers the NSW Open, Seve Ballesteros the Australian PGA title, and Gary Player capturing the Tooth's Classic up on the Queensland Gold Coast at the Tweed Heads — Coolangatta Golf Club.

An impressive list of winners, I am sure you will agree. The players were all well aware of the manner in which overseas visitors had plundered our circuit (and good luck to them) and needed no reminding of the fact in the unflattering terms employed by Peter Thomson. In his published ridicule of Australia's hopes of keeping the title at home Thomson (who is president of the Australian PGA) declared that I was 'a shadow of my former self' as well as making other uncomplimentary remarks about Jack Newton, Stewart Ginn and even his old mate Kel Nagle, whom he declared to be suffering from 'old age.' I found his remarks highly offensive, and from my observations he seems to take every opportunity to have a go at Australians, whether it is in his newspaper articles or on television. Although I naturally do not get the opportunity to listen to his television remarks when I am playing, I understand from many of my viewing friends that he rarely has a good word for me.

It seems incredible that a man who knows what it is all about out there in the championship world should be greatly lacking in understanding. I do my best all the time, but he seems to be telling the public that I am not. Most of the other players agree with me that Thomson's television comments rarely recognize our efforts and performances. One fact that he should keep in mind is that I have played all over the world in the past few years, and have beaten stronger fields than I usually encounter in Australia, and that applies to many other of my contemporary Australians.

I spoke openly and at length to the Australian Press about my reaction to Thomson's criticism, and it was given a good deal of exposure. It certainly got my hackles up for the championship ahead, and when I read Thomson's reaction to my reply next day I wondered just how much tongue-in-cheek was behind his original statement.

'I am pleased Greg's hackles are up. I hope it needles him into winning. There is nothing I would like more than to see him prove me wrong. I think it should be left at that.'

That may have been a clever justification in Thomson's mind for his insult to a big group of Australian players who felt strongly that their public image had been harmed by an unnecessary swipe at their ability.

After his victory in the NSW Open three weeks earlier Bill Rogers headed back to the U.S. for a fortnight's rest and a little quail-shooting. He came back to Melbourne refreshed and ready for the fray, and in the end took home the Australian Open. And if anybody was guilty of aiding and abetting his success then it was Greg Norman ... and a slippery, sandy stance on the tee of the 13th hole in the final round.

I will talk about that 13th teeing ground later on, but before I do let us recall the first three rounds of the tournament where Rogers fired three superb scores of 71, 69, 69 and stood seven under for the tournament with myself in second place four shots behind after scores of 71, 70, 72. My total of 213 was three better then par, and poised just a shot behind me were Gary Player, Graham Marsh and Jack Newton. At the halfway mark it was Billy Dunk who led the field after two rounds of 68-71, and having overcome his aversion to the big ball, was right on target for his first victory in the title. It was in the second round that Newton played one of the most unforgettable shots of his career — unforgettable not for brilliance but for exactly the opposite reason.

The first hole at Victoria is 256 yards and quite reachable, but as Jack got to the start of his downswing with his first shot of the second round a fly flew into his eye and he skied the ball 25 yards to the right and level with the ladies tee. It was an amazing sight to see the crowd on the first tee lift their eyes skyward and then turn to watch the flight of the ball. It went nowhere. All the gallery had to do to watch Jack play his second shot was an about-turn, and if Newton was slightly embarrassed about it all he was also determined to get it right this time. His father, Jack Newton senior, the Sydney policeman who caddies for his son when the tour reaches Australia, slung Jack's bag over his shoulder and walked the few yards to the ball, muttering, 'I can't bloody believe it! He hits putts that long.'

But Newton retrieved his position by slamming a 3 iron to the green and making his par four en route to a second round of 71 and a share of second place with Bill Rogers, a shot behind Dunk.

Next day Dunk ballooned to an 82, completely disappearing from contention, and Newton, suffering from a virus, fought pluckily for a 74 and went home to bed. He was never a threat after the third round.

Although Rogers went into the last day of the tournament four shots clear of me, he was aware that the tournament was by no means over, and confided in friends, 'Anything can happen. Norman and Marsh both think they still have a chance — just one double swing could do it.' How right he was! I went to the turn in 33, and when Rogers turned in 37 I had drawn level. I started back with three pars, and believed I had Rogers covered, as the American par-machine of the first three days was showing distinct signs of wear and tear.

But then came the 13th hole. The club had extended the teeing ground by a few feet for the championship, laying new turf to eke out every extra foot of distance it could, and the tee markers were back on that sandy, still unconsolidated area for the final day.

The hole measures 431 yards with a blind tee shot over a hill, but a generous landing area for the properly struck shot. Too far left and a tree-line blocks out the second shot, and too far right there was plenty of rough and ti-tree bushes to make life uncomfortable.

When I walked onto the tee I was shocked. I was confronted with a teeing ground that was soft and loose. The turf had not set properly and for some time I searched around for a teeing position that would give me a solid footing. I could not find one.

I rely a lot on my leg action for my power, and without a firm footing I have a tendency to slip, and because I could not get that firm footing on that final day at Victoria I believe I paid a huge price. I elected to hit a 1 iron for safety. Just hit it down the middle and make par.

As I came down into the ball the inevitable happened — my right foot slipped from under me, and I hooked the ball so far left that I was blocked out for my second shot.

I was fuming as I left the tee. In the gallery I saw the club president, Mr John Westacott — a man I consider a good friend, but I am afraid he took the brunt of my anger. 'You bastards have no idea of putting tee positions down. If this costs me the Australian Open, then I am going to blame you guys,' I told him. In calmer moments after the tournament we sat down and discussed the cause of my anger. It certainly was not his fault personally, but I just needed somebody to whom I could fly off the handle, and poor John Westacott was the man who just happened to be there.

One disaster followed another down that 13th hole. My second shot went through the trees to the right rough, from whence I missed the green with a sand iron. I chipped my ball badly, and faced a twelve-footer to save a bogey. The putt was vital, but when it lipped out a double bogey 6 went on my card just at the time I least needed it.

I still believed I had plenty of holes left to win the title, but when birdies eluded me at the next two holes I was starting to get desperate. While I was piling one blunder onto another at the 13th I heard the gallery back on the 12th explode into a roar of applause, and I did not have to be told that Rogers had birdied and taken the lead again.

When I got to the short 16th I told my caddie, 'I have to go for it.' The flag was tucked in on the left of the green, and I hit a 3 iron as well as I have ever hit any golf-shot. It finished four feet from the hole, and when I made the putt for a birdie I was back in the thick of it.

Behind me Rogers bogeyed the 13th and 14th, and when he could manage only another bogey at the 16th we were level with two holes to play. That slippery calamity back on the 13th was assuming greater importance now, but I told myself that a birdie at the final hole would at least get me into a play-off … just get the four, and let Rogers do the worrying.

The hole is 507 yards long, and with the adrenalin running I smashed my last drive over 360 yards down the fairway. I believe they still talk about it at Victoria.

When I got to the ball my caddie and I did a quick reckoning on our yardage chart and came up with the same answer — it was 142 yards to the front of the green. 'It is a wedge,' I said.

In retrospect that was the only club I thought of hitting, and I knew I had to hit the ball right of the big bunker guarding the left of the green and pitch it on the front. I had a slightly hanging lie, and the ball left the club-face on a line that I immediately knew was wrong.

Had I hit it hard enough to carry the sand trap? For what seemed an eternity the ball hovered high in the air, right on line with the flag. It fell just short and into the sand. Now I had to get down in two for the birdie I so badly needed. My sand-iron shot ran 12 feet by the hole. It was an uphill putt sliding left to right, and I was calmly confident that I would still make it — but I didn't. It lipped out, and I was well aware that I had left the gate open for Bill Rogers.

The American slipped through that opening quite comfortably, hitting a 4 iron home for his second and getting down in two putts for the title. As he came down the 18th Laura and I were sitting in the front seat of the stands holding hands, both well aware that in a few moments my Australian Open crown would pass to another head. When Rogers holed out he walked over to us and said, 'How did you make five down there?' When I told him I had pumped a drive so far down the fairway that I only needed a pitching wedge for my second he replied incredulously, 'You hit a wedge for your second? I can't believe that.' Although at the time the wedge was all I could think of perhaps I was in error. My strategy had been to hit the wedge to the front of the green and let the ball run down towards the hole, and if it had worked I believe I would have had a reasonable putt for an eagle.

Perhaps a 9 iron would have been the correct shot. Perhaps I should have hit that club, and gambled on two putts from the back of the green. Golf has always been a game of what might have been, and if only …

For Bill Rogers his victory in the Australian Open capped a truly remarkable year. He had won seven tournaments, including the British Open title, and his victories had been achieved in four different countries. The man was on the hottest winning streak of any player in the world that year.

For me thoughts of Metropolitan in 1979 crowded into my head. There was a very close comparison between what happened at Victoria, and what had happened at Metropolitan two years earlier. Both times the final hole of the tournament had cruelly brought about my downfall. In the space of three Opens I had been successful once and twice runner-up, and a chance to emulate the record of the late Ossie Pickworth had slipped from my grasp. Pickworth is the only man in the history of the Open championship to win in three successive years, and I still have plenty of time to equal his record.

I hope I can. I dearly want to prove Peter Thomson wrong.

CHAPTER 16
THE EUROPEAN TOUR

Despite the loss of my Australian Open championship, 1981 had been a highly successful year for me, both on and off the golf-course. My tournament earnings were close to the $250,000 mark again, and off the course other business interests were coming together nicely.

Since our wedding back in July most of the time Laura and I had spent together had been used up chasing one golf tournament after another, and living out of suitcases on either side of the Atlantic. Because we had never had a proper honeymoon, I had plans to right that wrong by taking Laura cruising and fishing along the Queensland coast, and as we flew out of Melbourne the disappointment of my championship loss was quickly pushed from our minds as we both looked forward to a long holiday from golf at Paradise Point.

For the next month or so my golf-clubs would stay in the corner. We spent a couple of days preparing for sea, loading provisions and getting our honeymoon cruiser ship-shape for the three weeks we planned to be away.

I had picked out the places along the coast where we would call in to refuel, and we cast off in high spirits, but it was only a few days before I changed course 180 degrees and headed back to Paradise Point.

Poor Laura! She tried bravely to share my love of the sea, but our honeymoon cruise was not the idyllic experience we had hoped it would be. I will let you into a secret. She gets seasick, and those waves of nausea hit her hardest when I stopped the boat to fish, and it rocked around gently in the slop. I teased her about it, but seasickness is no joke, and if you have ever experienced it you will know what I mean.

Christmas was approaching, and my parents and my sister Janis and her husband Glen Wedge (yes, Wedge) and their two children came down from Brisbane to celebrate with us. It was Laura's first time as hostess to her new Australian family, and she served up a Christmas dinner fit for a king.

I had plenty of time to reflect on the year as I lazed around the pool and soaked up the sunshine at Paradise Point in those few precious weeks away from the tour. Sometimes friends would call in, and it gave me a lot of pleasure to stoke up the barbecue out on the back lawn and cook steaks and sausages while we enjoyed a beer.

Earlier in the year I had won the Australian Masters title at Huntingdale in Melbourne, and shortly afterwards gone to America for my first tilt at the U.S.

Masters. My fourth placing there had certainly brought me to the notice of the American public, but it was when I flew the Atlantic to tackle the European tour once again that the cash register started its healthy ring.

Europe, and more particularly England, has always been a happy hunting-ground for me, and it is the years that I have put in on that circuit that have really taught me how to win.

There are many professional golfers in this world endowed with great shot-making ability who have yet to learn how to convert opportunity into victory when the chance arises, and I am afraid many of them are in Britain.

From 1984 onward I plan to play most of my golf on the American tour, and if I prove successful in that environment it will be because playing in Europe has taught me so much. It has taught me that there is only one yardstick for measuring a man's ability — victory. No player can tee up and win every tournament he plays in. It would be ridiculous to think he could. But there is a barrier that separates real winners from those players who go along each week to make up the field.

In the years that I have played the European tour it is not unfair to say that Seve Ballesteros, Bernhard Langer and myself have pretty well dominated the tournament scene, along with a handful of Britishers. What concerns me about British golf is its failure to produce a player in the Superstar category, in the mould of a Jack Nicklaus or a Lee Trevino or a Tom Watson. Tony Jacklin did it a dozen years ago, but since then there has been nobody.

Why? One popular theory is that the British Press expects too much of their

126

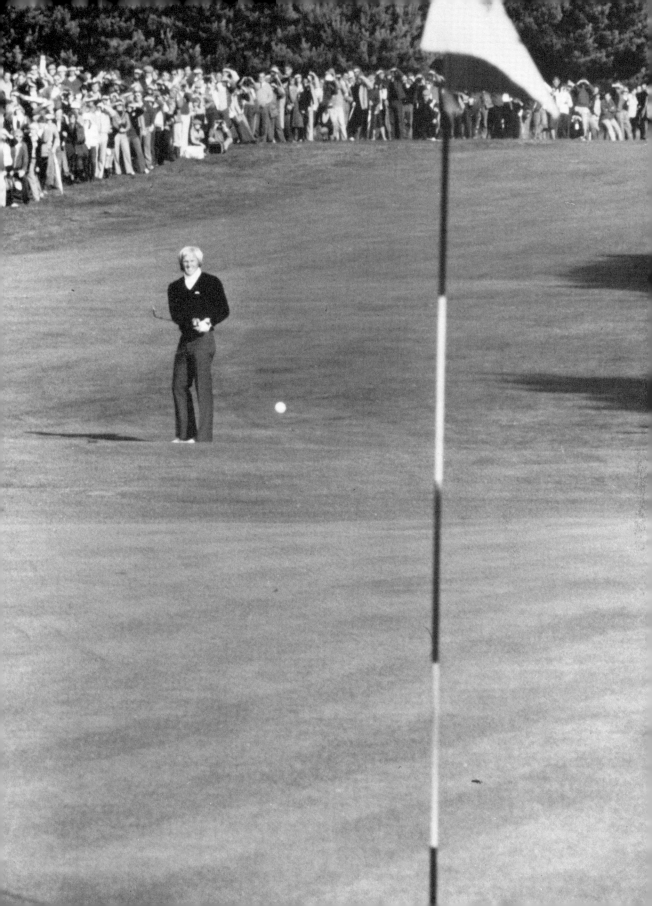

home players, predicting great things for them, and when they do not produce, damning them with a ferocity that produces only inferiority complexes.

That is a theory to which I do not subscribe fully. The British golf-writing corps reflects a national disappointment when its players fail, and that is their duty. The fault lies with the players themselves, who are too often content to run second, or tenth, or anywhere that will earn them a good cheque without going through the mentally or physically demanding rigours of actually winning. Of course, there are exceptions, and I name Sandy Lyle and Nick Faldo as a couple of them, while that farming veteran Neil Coles is another. So is Sam Torrance. Among my very best friends in professional golf are many of the players I am talking about, so that I feel competent to make those observations I am making, while at the same time hoping to retain those friendships.

So many talented golfers on the British tour have not got the drive, have not got the guts or that inner power that is needed to go on and win when victory is in sight. The desire is there, but the raw courage to turn that desire into a reality is sadly missing. There are too many good-time players in the British tour who would be better off spending their spare time on the practice fairway, honing their skills to the point where they can stand up under pressures that winning a golf tournament demands. Nobody can do it for them. They have to do it themselves.

I find the practice fairways around the British tour very lonely places, because quite often I am the only one there. I make it a ritual to go to the practice ground after every tournament round I play — good or bad — because it is only there that any problems that have arisen during the day can be sorted out.

In the past year or so this trend has been slowly changing, and although the practice fairways are never crowded in the late afternoons a few more players are becoming aware of their importance.

If I do find somebody to talk to on the practice fairway quite often it is Ken Brown, because if there is a player with real dedication in Britain, then it is Ken. But he still remains the enigma of the tour. I am a great admirer of this string-bean Scot whose tea-cosy headwear and slow play make him a prominent and controversial figure on the tour.

Brown has a mental attitude that refuses to recognize the skill in his hands. If ever a man has talked himself out of a fortune it is Brown, and I have told him so. Often I have seen him grind out scores that have put him in a position to win a tournament, and then back away because he tells himself that he cannot do it.

He did it at Royal Melbourne a few years ago in the Australian PGA title, where he led the tournament for three rounds and then drifted out of contention, finally ending up with a two-shot penalty for slow play and a last round of 81.

On the first three days around the composite course at Royal Melbourne his scores were 68, 71, 70, and those superb rounds gave him a three-stroke lead going into the last round. At the end of each day Ken would reluctantly face Australia's golf-writers and tell them, 'Really, I have no chance of winning.'

His pessimism reflected the man, and true to his word he fired a final round of 79, topped off by a two-shot penalty for slow play. Sam Torrance won the tournament, but I hope you see what I mean about poor Ken. What an attitude!

I once played a tournament round in England with Ken and Nick Faldo when we were all fined for slow play. Ken was on the receiving end of the heaviest

128

penalty, but while we were sitting around waiting to hear our fate I told him that unless he changed his habits he would destroy himself on the golf-tour. I told him that other players on the tour would grow to hate playing with him, and would not want to be involved with him. 'You will ruin your own golf game,' I told him. And he replied, 'I cannot help it.' I am afraid he is developing into a tragic figure in the game, and it is not so long ago that he jumped the fence at one tournament and ran away from a Press conference he should have attended. I feel sorry for him, and for the way he is crucifying his career. If he is going to alter his public image then he should do it quickly — for his own sake, and for the sake of British golf. He must adopt a more carefree attitude, and even if he is not enjoying himself try and give the impression that he is.

My advice to Ken is to be nice to people, even if he feels it would kill him, otherwise his life in golf could be prematurely cut short. He has a big following in the game, but the way he is isolating himself from the media is doing him a lot of damage, because once you do that then you are virtually cutting yourself off from the public that supports golf.

In Britain the climate does not allow for year-round golf as it does in Australia or the United States, but if the top British players — and the lesser ones, for that matter — looked more closely at the Australian and New Zealand spring and summer tours they would find plenty to attract them.

Unfortunately, the Australasian tour clashes with the South African circuit. Although I have never played the South African tour, I am sure the quality of golf courses and the quality of competition would not compare with what is offered in Australia.

Many of the British players who go to South Africa have told me that they go there for a good time, and play the golf tournaments to finance what amounts to a holiday for them. I realize the great difference in the cost of travelling to South Africa and in the cost of flying to Australia, but the prize money in our major tournaments is far greater.

I think my persuasive powers could have been behind the decision of Eamonn Darcy, John O'Leary and Sam Torrance to make recent visits Down Under, and I am sure none of them have regretted it. I would dearly like to see more British golfers come out in future years and play our great golf-courses, because I believe it would not only inject interest in our Australian tournaments but also help to lift the standard of British golf. Because the British tour has been so good to me, I make the suggestion for what it is worth.

Although I said earlier that the British golf-scene causes me concern, there are one or two bright young stars on the horizon.

In 1982 Gordon Brand junior achieved a feat that no other British rookie has ever managed by winning two tournaments on the European tour. He won at Porthcawl, where I was runner-up, and then came out and captured the Bob Hope Classic at Moor Park. His two successes are just the sort of shot in the arm that the British tour needs, and it will be fascinating to watch his progress over the next few years.

When I reached London in the May of 1981 I made a cheeky prediction that I was back in the UK to win three tournaments in a row, and although that did not quite happen I went very close to doing it.

I have said before that Wentworth is one of my favourite courses, and after the way it treated me in the Martini International again it was even closer to my

Winner of the Martini International for the third time at Wentworth, England in 1981.

heart. Two years earlier I had won the Martini title over the 'Burma Road', and in 1980 it was Wentworth again where I captured the World Match Play championship.

All the omens were on my side. My two previous victories in the Martini had been in 1977 and 1979, and as this was another 'odd' year my stars were in the right quarter. And so it proved.

I believe, though, that it was the manner of that victory that really captured the imagination, because no script-writer could have dreamed up a more spectacular finish than the one that took me to the narrowest of victories over Germany's Bernhard Langer.

The course was waterlogged for most of the tournament, but when it got down to the 'crunch' holes the title swung my way.

Rain caused several long delays during the final round, which I started two shots away from the leader, fellow-Australian Noel Ratcliffe. I was playing in the second last group, with Langer, Ratcliffe and Roger Davis in the final group, and we were out on the course for almost six hours.

The last two holes at Wentworth are both par fives, and when I reached the 17th tee I knew the whole tournament was on a knife-edge, and that something very special was needed over the last two holes. I birdied the 17th, and then muscled a big drive down the last hole.

The saturated fairway stopped the ball almost where it landed, and I still had a long way to go to the hole. 'You need an eagle to make sure,' my caddy told me as we stood together in the middle of the fairway, pondering what club to hit. I took a 1 iron out of the bag and sent the ball soaring 228 yards and 18 feet from the hole, pin-high. When I tapped it home for an eagle it left Langer with a birdie to tie, and when he failed from 15 feet I had won my third Martini.

The victory itself was very satisfying, but the manner in which it was achieved was something I will never forget. A birdie-eagle finish to win by a shot really is something you only dream about. My total of 287 was the only score under par for the tournament, but the incredible weather conditions were the main reason for the high scoring that week.

As Michael Williams commented in the London *Daily Telegraph*, I had 'timed my sprint to perfection'. The first leg of the treble I had forecast on my arrival had been duly achieved, but at Ganton the following week I could manage only fourth place in the Sun Alliance PGA title, finishing seven shots behind Nick Faldo. Faldo finished 10 under par on 274, to take the event by four shots from Neil Coles and Ken Brown, while I was a further three shots behind on 281.

There were plenty of players ahead of me when I shot a level par 72 in the first round of the Dunlop Masters at Woburn the following week, but it was a different story at the end of the fourth day.

My next three rounds produced some of the best golf I have ever played in Britain, as I shot 68, 66, 67 to finish on 273, 15 under par. It gave me a four-shot victory over Graham Marsh, and it was probably the first time ever that Australians have finished first and second in a major title in Britain.

Marsh matched my final round of 67, and said later, 'I knew that for me to win Greg would have to have an ordinary day. Instead he made another great score and even with my own 67 I did not have a dog's chance.' And in a tribute that I value he added, 'I guess that Greg is the longest, straightest driver in golf — and that is some start to give the boy.'

I had fallen just short of that optimistic prediction I had made a month earlier but two out of three was quite gratifying and the £27,000 ($50,000) represented a healthy boost to the Norman coffers.

There was another element in that wonderful three weeks in Britain about which I told nobody, but I was very conscious of its importance.

Two years earlier at the Metropolitan golf club in Melbourne I had missed a four-footer on the last green to tie with Jack Newton in the Australian Open championship. At the time I was bitterly disappointed, and in searching for a scapegoat concentrated my wrath on the putter I had used.

It was the putter I had used back in my amateur days, and when it failed me at Metropolitan in that moment of crisis I decided to banish it forever. But on the flight to London I got to thinking about that old friend-turned-foe, and decided it was time for a reconciliation. I telephoned my mother as soon as I reached England and asked her to pack it carefully and air-mail it over to me. She knew exactly to which corner of the house I had condemned it, and by the time the Martini started that old putter and I were back together again. It arrived four days before the tournament began, and as soon as I had it back in my hands again I felt happy. I decided to forgive it for its misbehaviour at Metropolitan, and by the way it behaved for me in the next three weeks I do believe it was trying to say sorry too.

After my Masters victory Ron Wills in the London *Daily Mirror* declared, 'Norman is not only a successful player. He has taken over from Severiano Ballesteros as the darling of the crowds. And, unlike the Spaniard the big fair-haired Australian always has time for a wave and a smile — whether he has just birdied a hole or just dropped a shot … .'

It was earlier that year that I had spent a lot of time thinking about what I wanted to get out of life, and just where I was headed. I do not think I have ever shrunk from a positive analysis of my own abilities, and I believe I have what is required to aim for the No. 1 spot in world golf. This belief has changed my whole approach to golf, and I am a far more positive player than I ever was.

In all sports — and more particularly in golf — one must have a consuming belief in one's own skills, allied to a strength of character that will fuse those ingredients for success in the very highest level of competition. It is the skill and the mental make-up of Jack Nicklaus and Tom Watson that make them the great players they are.

I am very conscious that I have never won a major title, never won the British Open, the U.S. Masters, the U.S. PGA or the U.S. Open, and until I do then I will not believe that I have successfully brought together those ingredients for greatness that I have mentioned.

Opposite
The stresses and strains of championship golf: 1981 Dunlop Masters at Woburn, England.

…. and the rewards. Receiving the trophy and cheque from the Duke of Bedford after winning the 1981 Dunlop Masters.

Shortly after I arrived in England I was delighted to study a world ranking of professionals compiled most diligently by a leading golf magazine that had me in eighth place. The year before I had been ranked 38th by the same panel of judges, comprising golf-writers from both sides of the Atlantic and other parts of the globe. As the magazine editor, Peter Haslam, explained, over a thousand players had been considered to find the top fifty players in the world, and to find myself in eighth place after just five years on the professional tour was a good indication of my progress.

I played only nine tournaments on the European tour in 1981, and won altogether a total of £51,017 or close to $90,000. I had a stroke average of 70·57, and despite my limited number of tournaments still managed to finish in fourth place on the official money list. In the course of my many visits to Britain I have often been approached to lend my name to companies or organizations anxious to have a player representing them on the European tour, but until now I have resisted most of these offers because I felt that representing Australia was all the identification I needed.

During the Dunlop Masters at Woburn I was introduced to John Pinner, who was representing a new golf complex called Rolls of Monmouth.

It transpired that the course is on a property once owned by the Rolls family, of Rolls-Royce fame. The course has been built on the home park of the Hendre estate, which was the home of C.S. Rolls, and in time to come it will be a full-stretch championship test of 6,701 yards, parred at 72. The present owner of the complex is Mr John Harding, and after several talks I agreed to represent the new complex as their playing professional in Europe.

Eventually the original stately Hendre mansion will be refurbished to serve as the clubhouse for members, but at the time of writing the spacious brick outbuilding employed by C.S. Rolls during the early development of the Rolls-Royce engine, and later to house the full range of cars belonging to the Rolls family, is being used by the membership.

Part of my deal with Rolls of Monmouth is that I drive a Rolls-Royce car, and I can assure you I am finding no hardship in doing that.

CHAPTER 17
MY BEST INVESTMENT

Like any other sportsman, I am very conscious of the important role the public plays in the support of my chosen profession, but there are times when I desperately need to escape from the crowded golf-scene.

Basically I am a very private person, and away from the hectic arena of international golf I enjoy nothing more than the company of my family and friends. These are the people who understand me and my shortcomings, and to whom I can relate readily — people who do not dwell on missed putts or poor rounds but are more likely to hand me a tea-towel and tell me to dry the dishes.

I would not have it any other way.

I have mentioned earlier the door-bangers who had started to worry us at our beachfront home in Paradise Point, and by now it was quite obvious that the peace and seclusion I thought I had bought there was a myth. In many ways the attention was flattering, but it also became a worry, and early in 1982 Laura and I decided that the best course of action was to sell the beachfront property and establish ourselves in another home on the Gold Coast of Queensland.

We also considered several other factors before we finally reached the decision to sell. The maintenance of my new sea-going cruiser was almost a full-time job, and as we were away for most of the year it would be foolish indeed to leave her tied up at the jetty unused and uncared for. I had bought this boat to replace the old *Divot II*, and had not owned it for long before we decided to put both the house and the boat on the market.

My last sea journey in *Divot II* was an experience I am not likely to forget in a hurry, and it possibly influenced me to part with her.

Deep-sea fishing has always been a passionate love of mine, and during my break from tournament commitments in early 1982 I planned a novel fishing competition which included my close friend Cyril King and his three sons Greg, Gary and Steve.

The idea was for Cyril and Steve to stay on Moreton Island, just off the Queensland coast, and fish, while Greg, Gary and I headed for the open sea after bigger game. Because we anticipated bigger fish we gave Cyril and Steve a 4-1 start — in other words, if we caught a sixteen-pounder then all they had to do to match that was to catch a fish weighing four pounds.

We put out to sea from Moreton Island in high spirits, and confident we could

My home in Queensland, Australia, a few miles inland from the famous Gold Coast.

win our little competition, but in fact no decision was ever to be reached, and no winners ever declared.

I gave *Divot II* close to full throttle, and she purred through the water beautifully until we reached a position about ten or fifteen miles off the coast, and due east of Glasshouse Mountain. I took a fix on this landmark, and then we dropped anchor and settled down to enjoy our fishing.

We had anchored in about 350 feet of water, right on the edge of the Continental Shelf, and in a spot where I knew from experience that good-size fish abounded. I had fished them scores of times without incident, and while Greg and Gary cast their lines I went into the cabin to open a small bottle of beer for each of them to enjoy while they sat and waited for a bite.

There was no warning as the huge wave came crashing across the stern of the *Divot II*.

Through the flying spray and crashing water Gary was hurled from his position on the starboard side of the boat and thrown heavily into the engine-casing. The bottle of beer I had just opened went flying from my hand as *Divot II* went into convulsions, dipping her portside gunwale dangerously deep into the angry seas.

Self-preservation was uppermost in each of our minds as we grabbed desperately for any fixture that would stop us from being swept overboard. Slowly, ever so slowly, *Divot II's* portside broke free of the clutching waters as

136

she fought to right herself. The fact that she was a self-draining cruiser certainly saved her from turning turtle on us, and as she got herself back to the perpendicular I asked both Greg and Gary, 'Are you O.K.'? They assured me they were, but Gary was going to carry a few bruises and abrasions for a time, and apart from each of us being saturated and shaken (and more than a little scared), we had all come through the ordeal safely. However, it had certainly killed our enthusiasm for fishing so we decided to declare the competition no contest and weigh anchor and head back to Moreton Island.

A fortnight later I sold *Divot II*, and Laura and I went house-hunting.

We looked at several properties, but turned them all down for one reason or another until one day a real-estate friend of mine called and told me about an almost new house inland from Surfers Paradise. 'I think you will like this one. It has just come onto the market,' he said. When we saw the house both Laura and I fell in love with it immediately. It was a large 'neo-Colonial' style home on five acres of land with a separate guest suite, four bedrooms and a swimming-pool.

There was one other feature that attracted me. One boundary fence was much longer than the others, and I saw straight away that I had enough space to build my own practice fairway.

'I can hit anything up to a 5 iron down that side,' I said to Laura.

We bought the house.

Our new home offered us contrasting attractions to those at Paradise Point,

It is a luxury to have one's own practice fairway so why not make good use of it? I can hit a full 5-iron shot down the length of one of my boundary fences and get a sun-tan at the same time. If the Queensland sun gets too hot, then I use beach umbrellas to shield me and keep on hitting golf balls.

137

where the daily pelican parade and the ready fishing were a constant source of pleasure. Now we had wallabies and kangaroos and a magnificent collection of multi-coloured bird life to attract our attention.

We were anxious to move in as soon as we could, but before we could do that I was contracted to play in two events in Melbourne, the Victorian Open championship and the Australian Masters title which I was defending.

Once again the Victorian Open was to be staged around my nemesis, Metropolitan — a course which holds bad memories for me, and one on which I have played many major tournaments without ever winning. For several years now the organizers of this event have hinged it around a 'Celebrity Guest' formula, and the man who filled the role in 1982 was the great Supermex, Lee Trevino. He was following in the footsteps of many famous players on the American tour when he arrived in Melbourne, and like all his predecessors he went home without the title.

Among the players who have been brought to Melbourne for this tournament in past years, and have failed to take it away with them, are Johnny Miller, Gary Player, Ben Crenshaw, Curtis Strange and Arnold Palmer, so Trevino was in exalted company, and should not have been over-worried about his failure.

The Victorian Open is staged at the height of the Southern Hemisphere summer, and quite often we play in temperatures close to 100 degrees. Nevertheless, it is a tournament that exudes atmosphere and if it gets too hot, why, there is a nice big lake beside the 11th fairway, and it is not uncommon for members of the paying public to dive in and cool off.

Trevino is always a huge attraction, and with him topping the bill, and the best Australian players in the field striving to cut him down, all the ingredients for a great tournament were there. Besides, he was making his first appearance in Melbourne since 1974, when he hit the world headlines by describing the greens at Royal Melbourne's composite course as the 'biggest joke since Watergate'. Trevino said after his Royal Melbourne experience that he would never play on the course again, and he has repeated that statement often over the years. It is a pity, because Royal Melbourne forgave him long ago, and would love to have him back there. He was playing in a Chrysler Classic at the time of his 'Watergate' outburst, and claims that he made the statement because he believed the lightning-fast greens were unfair.

Now the action for Trevino's return visit to Melbourne was across town at Metropolitan and when he fired opening rounds of 70, 68 to lead the field at the halfway mark it seemed just possible that he might break the hoodoo that every Celebrity Guest seems to have at this tournament. At this stage of the tournament I was seven shots behind him, but when I got it all together in the third round for 68 and Trevino took 73 I was back in the thick of the fight.

Bob Shearer was the pacemaker on 5 under par 211 with a round to play after putting together scores of 69, 71, 71, while alongside me on 213 was 'rookie' Mike Clayton, who had been a member of Metropolitan all his amateur life. He had turned professional only a few months prior to this tournament, and the week before had holed in one at the last hole of the Tasmanian Open title to pick up a useful $5,000 cheque.

One of the many side-bar attractions to the Victorian Open was a $20,000 cash prize for a hole in one at the club's 13th hole, and on the third day of the tournament young Clayton's excellent first two rounds had earned him a draw alongside Billy Dunk and Trevino.

Before the trio got to the 13th hole Dunk and Trevino had made a pact that if either of them were lucky enough to 'ace' the hole, then they would share the spoils equally. They did not bother to include Clayton. He had holed out just the week before, and could not possibly do it again.

Clayton said later, 'I'm glad they did not ask me. It would have cut my profit by two-thirds.' He was to stand on the 13th and slam a 3 iron right down the throat of the hole, so that in the space of a week he collected hole-in-one prizes worth $25,000. What a way to start a professional golf career!

But that was not all. He went on to win the tournament, and another $20,000.

The shock of that ace in the middle of his third round did not help Clayton's concentration, even if it was a big boost to his scorecard. He finished with a 74, but on the last day stood up under tremendous pressure to shake off a field of far more experienced and tournament-toughened players, to win by three shots from Bob Shearer.

Clayton's total of 281 was 7 under par, and his final round of 68 left us all in the young man's wake. I had started the day on level terms with him, and although I rejoiced for him in his great moment I was not amused with my own performance. If he had been in a winning position, obviously then so had I, but while he shot 68 I piled up a 75, and fell away to a level par total of 288. Certainly I had not played a tournament for ten weeks, but that was no excuse. I stayed up all night in my hotel room after that tournament practising my putting across the carpet and sitting on the edge of the bed, going over and over that last round.

My final analysis for my failure was that my thinking on the course had been poor, and that I had not applied myself to the task with the intensity necessary to win. Time and again I went through the round, shot by shot, until I finally slipped between the sheets as dawn was breaking.

I have said before that self-analysis of failure is a strict part of my approach to tournament golf, and although I considered that I had worked out the problems that had beset me at Metropolitan, I was not able to correct them by the time I teed up in defence of my Australian Masters title a few days later. The course on which this tournament is played — Huntingdale — is a man-sized layout in anybody's language, and although I won the event the year before by seven shots, I had many outside influences on my mind in 1982. Instead of concentrating my attention on the tournament I am afraid my mind kept wandering to our new home in Queensland. Both Laura and I were anxious to return north and move in.

I eventually finished in 8th place after being in quite a sound position at the halfway mark with two rounds of 73, but instead of going forward from that point I went backward.

The title was won by Graham Marsh, and it was good to see him finally break through in one of our majors. Despite his enormous successes around the world, Marsh had never been able to capture a major four-rounder in Australia until this title came his way after a thrilling tussle over the last few holes with my close friend Stewart Ginn.

For most of my early years in professional golf I had been managed by English businessman Mr James Marshall, but as I became more used to the cut and thrust of the business negotiations in the professional game, and more familiar with the intricacies of contractual arrangements, I considered I was capable of handling my own affairs. I felt, I daresay, that I had grown-up, and when Laura and I flew to England in early 1982 I resolved to tell Mr Marshall that I wanted to control my own affairs in the future. I told him of my decision during dinner at the Grosvenor House Hotel in London. From my viewpoint it was a perfectly natural progression in my career.

Now that I had taken what I considered a significant step I set out to justify it in the best way I knew how — with results — but early in 1982 I was really struggling for form on the European tour. In the early tournaments I played, I can only say that my performances were mediocre, and that most of my problems were linked to my putting. As that department of my game deteriorated so did the rest of my golf, and I slipped further and further into the 'horrors'.

Anyway, whatever the reasons, I found my confidence and my belief in myself at a lower ebb than they had ever been since I first turned professional. I felt desperate about my situation, and for the first time in my career desperate about the problems in my golf game, for which I could not find a solution.

During the Martini International at Lindrick in Yorkshire my game and spirits hit rock-bottom, and as I drove from the club after the final round I was determined to find a solution that would start swinging the pendulum in the reverse direction.

At the 17th hole in the final round I had taken 14 shots before I finally squeezed that pesky little golf ball into the hole for a closing 82. The tournament was won by Bernard Gallacher, a mammoth 19 shots ahead of my finishing total of 296.

Most people who play this game have suffered the ignominy of double figures, but it is a rare occurrence in top-flight professional golf. It was the highest single-hole score on the European tour for many a tournament and I was the subject of plenty of needle as a result.

It all started when I hooked my tee shot into trees and piled up a string of penalties as I tried vainly to recover back to the fairway. As I swished away in the trees I knew the gallery was getting a chuckle from my predicament, and once I had finished the hole I was able to see the amusing side of it too. Golf fans rarely see players run up cricket scores at a single hole, but although I could understand their amusement there was a serious message in that silly hole for me, because it was symptomatic of the problems I was facing every time I teed up.

In Melbourne a year earlier I had met Dr Rudi Webster, a West Indian who had played county cricket in England as a fast bowler for Warwickshire, and was close to selection for his country's Test XI several years earlier, besides managing the West Indian team during its World Series Cricket tours of Australia in the late 70's.

Dr Webster studied at Edinburgh University, where he took his degree in medicine, but for many years he has taken a close interest in sportsmen and their mental approach to their tasks. I first met him over a friendly drink and a meal in the Toc H hotel in the fashionable inner Melbourne suburb of Toorak, and was fascinated by his opinions and his understanding of the problems that plague every sportsman.

He told me how he had counselled the great Sir Garfield Sobers and Vivian Richards, and how he had convinced both men that they would be 'Superstars',

Opposite
Successfully defending my Dunlop Masters title at St Pierre Golf Club, Chepstow, Wales in 1982.

and he stressed that ridding the mind of disruptive mental influences was one of the real keys to sporting success. His involvement in sport is purely a hobby, and in this area he describes himself as a 'mental skills coach' rather than a 'motivator', although I dare say one is complementary to the other. He had been living and practising in Australia for nearly twelve years when I met him, and his telephone number in Melbourne is one that I now always keep close by me.

When I arrived back in London I told Laura of my problem, and the way I was thinking badly on the golf-course, and said to her, 'I think I will ring Rudi Webster. He may be able to help me.'

Laura and I rarely discuss golf, and I try to keep my on-course problems out of our daily conversation, but she was well aware of the way I was suffering. 'I think it is a great idea,' she said encouragingly.

It was in a mood of desperation that I phoned Dr Webster not long after Laura and I had settled into our hotel room and unpacked. For over half an hour I told him of my plight, and my real fears about the way my game was crumbling, and while I poured out my problems and their symptoms across 12,000 miles Dr Webster listened carefully. I told him of my lack of confidence, and how I believed I could not continue to play at the top level and do myself justice unless I regained that confidence quickly.

When I stopped my long — and I hope detailed — explanation of my problems Dr Webster calmly set about reassuring me, emphasizing that my mind and the way I controlled it on the golf-course was as important as any shot I might hit during the tournament. He told me to dispel my doubts and fears and always to think of golf, not in terms of numbers, but in terms of hitting the ball. When I put the telephone down I just sat for an hour and thought about the advice he had given me, and the more I thought about it the more it made sound common sense.

I followed his advice with devastatingly successful results in the weeks ahead.

In just over a week's time I was due to head for Chepstow in Wales to defend my Dunlop Masters title, and Dr Webster had given me a completely new outlook, a new philosophy, to take into the heat of battle, and I wanted to test it. I felt I was ready.

Before I made the trip to Wales Laura suggested that I supplement my telephone call to Dr Webster with several solid sessions on the practice ground, concentrating my attention on my short game. So for the next few days I drove every morning from London to Wentworth and worked my short irons for hours on end, punching wedges and 9 iron shots to fairway targets until I felt I had achieved a greater control over this department of my golf game than I ever had.

Sometimes I look back on that week at the beautiful St Pierre layout at Chepstow and point to it in my mind as a real landmark in my career. It had been over a year since I had won a tournament, and I needed a victory badly, not only to redeem myself in my own eyes but also to prove that I could rise above the upsets and distractions I had faced during that time.

I especially wanted to let the British public know that Greg Norman was still around and still capable of winning on the European circuit. It had been a long time between drinks.

After four days at Chepstow I walked off the last green not only with the Dunlop Masters title still beside my name but with it achieved in a manner that restored all my old confidence, and convinced me that the money I had spent

142

calling Dr Webster in Melbourne was probably the best investment I had ever made.

I won the title with rounds of 68, 69, 65, 65, and that added up to a whopping 17 under par total of 267, and the biggest winning margin in British golf for seventeen years.

I won by eight shots from Bernhard Langer, and no tournament in Europe had been won by a bigger margin since my own ten-shot win in the French Open two years earlier.

My talk with Dr Webster had not only jolted my mental processes into a more positive direction but it had also made me aware that I had lost my aggression on the golf-course. My negative thinking had made me play safe, and I am not that sort of golfer. I thrive on aggression, and love to attack, and that is exactly what I did at Chepstow.

But there is one other factor that I must not omit. The greens at Chepstow are truly among the best in the world, and the club turned them out at their immaculate best for the Dunlop Masters in 1982. That is not an observation made from the winner's rostrum, but one that was unanimously agreed to by every player in the tournament. They were magnificent.

When I was planning my schedule for 1982 I had originally planned to fly the Atlantic immediately the Dunlop Masters finished and tee up in the final pre-qualifying for the U.S. Open. I did not have an exemption into the tournament but dearly wanted to play, but at the last moment I was summoned to an urgent business meeting in London and was forced to forgo the trip to the United States.

I had been advised that it was impossible to change the dates of the London meeting, and so reluctantly I notified the United States Golf Association that I would not be in the final pre-qualifying for Pebble Beach. I wrote to the USGA and apologized for my absence and they wrote back, telling me that they understood the circumstances. It was a polite exchange, but I must say the next time I talked in public about the United States Golf Association I was a little more irate.

I believe firmly that the golf traffic across the Atlantic in June and July each year is too one-sided in favour of Americans and something should be done to redress that situation in fairness to the talent that now abounds on the European tour.

Each year the Americans exempt just one European player — the leader of the Official Money List — into the field for the US Open, but the list of exemptions extended by the Royal and Ancient to Americans is far more generous.

At the end of the year the top twenty players on the American tour plus ties are granted a start in the British Open if they wish to make the trip, and early in May of the current Open year the top three players (plus ties for third place) on the American tour are also exempt. So is the entire U.S. Ryder Cup team, and there are the usual exemptions for reigning and past champions that add to the imbalance of the player flow across the Atlantic.

There is no question that the influx of Americans to the British Open each year gives the old tournament a tremendous lift, but surely the USGA could be more expansive and grant four, or even six, players from Europe a place in their championship?

I do not think I made many friends when I voiced these opinions in mid-1982, and I know I was roundly criticized in the American magazine *Golf World* for my thoughts on the subject. It will not be long, I hope, before I am playing more and more of my golf in the United States, and I hope that by airing these opinions no prejudice is shown towards me.

As a matter of interest, I was interviewed on American television during the their PGA title in Tulsa won by Raymond Floyd and after I had explained the situation more fully many Americans agreed that I had made a valid point.

I made the point with the full understanding of the enormous pressure the USGA is under each year as thousands of hopefuls from all over the country attempt to play their way through a series of qualifying events, striving for a place in the great championship.

After my victory at Chepstow and the forced cancellation of my plans to play in the US Open at Pebble Beach I spent a frustrating week with nowhere to take my newly found streak of form. The Greater Manchester Open had been cancelled and I was virtually out of work, just at a time when I needed a tournament to test my momentum again.

CHAPTER 18
ENTER MISS NORMAN

I spent any slack period practising and then set off for the Coral Classic at Royal Porthcawl, where I finished second to one of the most promising 'rookies' we have uncovered on the European tour for years.

He is Gordon Brand junior — so named to distinguish him from his father of the same name, who is the club pro at the Knowle Club in Bristol, and also from another Gordon Brand on the tour.

Brand junior fired four rounds under par to beat me by three shots with a tournament total of 273, 15 under. I liked the way he handled himself in the tight situations throughout the tournament, and the young man was under a national microscope when he started the final round two shots clear of the field. His third round of 66 had elevated him to that position, and although I fired a final 67 Gordon's 68 was a closing performance that left us all in his shadow.

I think we were all impressed with young Brand's golf, and the former Walker Cup player looks certain to be a big influence on the European tour in the next few years. He has the perfect pedigree and background for the game, and as I did it myself, I understand the tremendous thrill he must have experienced in capturing a major event in his first professional year.

The only halfway cut I missed in Europe in the 1982 season was in the Scandinavian Open the following week in Sweden, but the cold, wet conditions were a miserable backdrop to a tournament to which I normally look forward eagerly.

Like the weather, my golf game was 'cold', and I returned to London determined not to be discouraged by that failure.

The Open championship was only a fortnight away now, and the immediate stepping-stone to the tournament was the State Express Classic at the Belfry, the headquarters of the British PGA in the English Midlands. The tournament was important for many reasons but mainly because it offered a place in the Open field to the top ten finishers who had not qualified through other avenues.

It was this attraction that brought the Americans Danny Edwards, Chip Beck and Rex Caldwell to the Belfry the week before the Open, and as Edwards was a former winner of the Greater Greensboro Open, the American challenge was very significant.

In fact, Edwards opened with two rounds of 68, 67 and for a brief time looked as if he would spreadeagle the field, but when he closed with a pair of 75's he

My 1982 U.K. successes
included the State Express
English Classic at The
Belfry *(opposite)* and the
Benson and Hedges
International at Fulford.

drifted back down the order into a share of seventh place. But he had secured his place in the Open field at Troon.

I eventually won the tournament with four consistent rounds of 70, 70, 70, 69, which gave me a shot to spare over Scot Brian Marchbank, who later told me that he had been playing so badly that he had considered not going to the Belfry. He won £8,000, so the change of mind was well worth his while.

That tournament had another special significance for Laura and me. It was the first time since we had been married over a year earlier that she had been in the gallery to see me win. Mind you, there had not been all that many successes, but it was a wonderful thrill for both of us. She told me later that she was so nervous at the last green that she could hardly watch me hole out, and there was a tear in her eye when I hugged her and said, 'That was for you.'

Before I leave the subject of the State Express English Classic I must tell you about a little challenge I accepted when I saw a plaque on the 10th green commemorating the fact that Seve Ballesteros had once driven his ball onto the putting surface.

The hole is 292 yards and downhill, with a lake guarding one side and the green partially hidden by tall trees. Seve had performed his feat in match-play back in 1978, and if he had failed to make the green then, why, the worst that could happen to him was to lose the hole. This was a stroke-play event, and consequently the punishment for failure could be so much greater. But in the second round of the Classic I decided to try and make the green from the tee, so I gave my driver a tremendous clout. To my great delight, and the delight of the big gallery, I found the target. What is more, I holed the putt from 20 yards for an eagle 2! Eat your heart out, Seve Ballesteros!

Laura and I drove from the Midlands to Royal Troon the following day, and I was quietly confident that I would make a better showing in the Open than I had managed in past years.

In my first practice round I joined with Jack Nicklaus, Tom Weiskopf and David Graham and achieved a 65 that collected all side bets, but when the serious business started two days later I could not reproduce that sort of scoring.

I have talked elsewhere about my feelings towards this great golf tournament, and do not plan to elaborate except to say that one day, hopefully, the breaks will go my way.

At Royal Troon I finished well down the order with rounds of 73, 75, 76, 72 for 296, and that sort of scoring certainly does not help pay the rent. America's Tom Watson captured the old trophy for the fourth time when he came home a shot ahead of the rank outsider, South African Nick Price, and expatriate Englishman Peter Oosterhuis. By Tom's own admission it was a 'default victory' because he had left the gate open for Price in that final round, but the inexperience of the South African told against him, and he stumbled badly when his success seemed assured.

Watson's winning total of 284 was just one better than that of Price, who totalled 285, but Watson was forced to wait nearly an hour in the clubhouse until he was certain he had won. He watched Price on television in the clubhouse making the blunders that were eventually to cost him the championship and hand the old trophy to the American.

In many ways it was an extraordinary tournament as young American Bobby Clampett charged ahead of the field on the first two days, bringing Royal Troon

148

to its knees with rounds of 67, 66. Just as he was being hailed as a first-year winner the old course took its cruel revenge and Bobby backed right off with closing rounds of 78, 77. His scores on the first two days were 11 under par, and on the second two days 11 over par — which is a very different way to finish level.

In professional golf the only thing to do to erase a bad performance from one's mind is to get on to the next tournament and play well. I pushed Royal Troon out of my mind as Laura and I flew the Atlantic, where I was scheduled to play the Canadian Open in Ontario and then the American PGA in Tulsa, Oklahoma.

I had my chances in both events, finishing 12th in the Canadian Open, and a challenging 5th behind Ray Floyd at Tulsa. My victory in the State Express English Classic had lifted me to the head of the European Money List, and I consolidated that position with a third placing in the Carrolls Irish Open and then a one-shot victory over Ian Woosnam, Bob Charles and Graham Marsh in the Benson and Hedges International in York.

It took a birdie at the final hole of the tournament to take the first-prize cheque away from them, and it was that win that made me believe I had an outside chance of heading the European Official Money List for the year. I say an outside chance because my entire playing schedule for Britain and Europe in 1982 included only eleven tournaments, and I was well aware that Sandy Lyle and Sam Torrance were planning a much fuller book than mine.

Laura and I had planned for our baby to be born in Orlando, Florida, close to her parents and to our new home, and after the Irish Open I flew back to Florida with her, while we moved in furniture, had curtains made and generally made ourselves comfortable. I do believe that the September-October period of 1982 were among the most hectic I have ever spent, as I crossed and recrossed the Atlantic six times in the space of four weeks.

Time changes meant nothing to me, as I treated the crossing as a daily commuter would treat his train ride into the office. Early in Laura's pregnancy we were told we could expect the baby to be born on 13 October and later this was amended to 20 October. Still later we were told to anticipate our new arrival on the original date of 13 October. I was getting a little confused, but I felt it was perfectly safe to fly to England in the first week of October to take part in a television series with Jan Stephenson, Beth Daniel and Bernhard Langer.

The matches were scheduled for three days at Woburn and when I booked into the Bell Inn in nearby Aylesbury I had no fears about being back to Orlando for the arrival of our baby.

On the first day of our mixed-sexes clash Langer and I were scheduled to play the two girls in a better-ball event over 9 holes with play starting at 9.30 a.m. I hit a few balls down the practice fairway and then strolled to the putting green for a few minutes' work on that department of my game, waiting for the call to the tee. But it was the telephone call from London that arrived first. 'It sounds quite urgent', the lass in the office told me as I hurried into the clubhouse. 'Hello,' I said. 'Greg Norman here.' 'It's John Davies, Greg. I have Laura on the other phone, and I think she has some news for you.'

John Davies is an amateur golfer of considerable skill, and we have been friends almost from the first visit I made to England in the late seventies.

My mind was racing. Why would Laura be phoning me at this time? Had anything gone wrong? Back in his London office John said calmly, 'Hang on and

150

you can talk to her.' He brought the two handsets together, earpiece to mouthpiece, and with this strange telephonic hook-up Laura told me that she was in hospital and in final labour. I was stunned. The baby timetable had really gone awry, and I was thousands of miles from her side.

I walked back to the tee with my head spinning and announced, 'I'm just about to become a father. It is eight days early.'

You may understand that I found it difficult to concentrate for the duration of the match, especially as the sponsors of our TV clash kept me in constant touch with Orlando in a rather unique way. Our match was backed by Cathay Pacific Airways, and for every step of the way a good friend of mine, Charlie Jack, was beside me with a walkie-talkie radio link to the clubhouse office. Every half-hour the office phoned the Orlando Hospital for a progress report on Laura, and then radioed Charlie Jack on the course.

Televised golf matches naturally take a good deal longer to play than a normal round of golf, but with my first child about to be born this one seemed like an eternity. I concentrated as hard as I could under the circumstances, but Langer and I were well beaten by the two girls.

Right through the day on the half-hour Charlie reported, and his news was always the same: 'No progress. Nothing has happened yet.'

The co-operation and assistance of everybody at Woburn that day was something I will never forget, but the day's golf ended without any of us knowing whether the baby had been born or not. I took up my own telephone inquiries when I returned to the Bell Inn later that afternoon, and when I got through to the hospital I was told that I would be able to speak to my wife in an hour or so. 'Yes. She had delivered the baby but Mrs Norman will talk to you in an hour.'

Laura had insisted that nobody but herself would tell me the news.

It was 6.00 p.m. English time when she was finally able to speak to me. 'Darling, we have a baby daughter,' she said.

It was 5 October 1982.

Morgan Leigh was just three months old when she posed for this picture with her Mum and Dad.

CHAPTER 19
MY GOLFING LIFE

We have named our daughter Morgan Leigh, and she is a thriving little bundle of joy for both of us.

It did not take long for everybody at the Bell Inn to realize I was a father. I told them all. That night an English businessman friend of mine, Billy Mullins, drove down from London and with Cathay Pacific's David Longmuir and Laurence Levy, now Morgan Leigh's godfather, helped me enjoy a quiet champagne celebration.

Jan Stephenson and Beth Daniel defeated Langer and myself 4-2 in the series, but I felt quite pleased with my performance under the rather difficult circumstances, winning both my matches against the girls.

The day after the baby was born was the last day of our commitment at Woburn, and I had already made plans for a quick exit from London.

Michael Hughesden's father is the chief executive of Leslie Godwin International Insurance and Reinsurance, one of the biggest companies of its type in the world, and as befitted a company of such importance it owned its own helicopter. Michael was able to make the company 'chopper' available to me, and as soon as the presentation had been completed at Woburn I climbed aboard, and in twelve minutes I was at Heathrow.

By car it would have taken over an hour.

Thirty minutes after I stepped out of the helicopter I was aboard Concorde bound for New York, where I picked up a connecting flight to Orlando almost immediately. Eight hours 50 minutes after lifting off from Woburn I was with Laura and Morgan Leigh in Orlando Hospital. My brother-in-law Jay was waiting for me at Orlando airport for the last leg of the journey, a journey where every connection had worked like clockwork. I doubt whether a single minute could have been shaved off the time. I felt like a twentieth-century Jules Verne.

In the few weeks we stayed in Orlando waiting for a medical clearance to allow Morgan Leigh to fly with us to Australia I was in negotiation with the Australian Golf Union to play in the Australian Open.

I sometimes believe that the subject of appearance money on the Australian golf scene is badly mishandled and the dealings our authorities had with David Graham and Bruce Devlin in 1982 have soured both those great players to a degree where they might not play tournament golf in their country of origin again.

While my negotiations with Australia were in progress I spent a lot of time on the fairways at the Bay Hill Country Club, just a few minutes from our home. Arnold Palmer is a part-owner of the club, and the real-estate development around it, and through him I have joined it, and use it frequently when we are at our Orlando house.

Except in the United States, I am paid appearance money everywhere I play, including Europe, Japan and Australia.

The only tournaments where I am not paid appearance money are the Martini International (which I have won three times) and the World Match Play championship (where all the invited players are on guarantees anyway). Because of the circumstances surrounding the financing of the 1982 Australian Open I agreed to play without an appearance fee, but I did negotiate a fee for playing two other tournaments in Australia. Once I had called off my negotiations for an appearance fee for the Australian Open I was looking forward keenly to playing in the event because, as you will recall, I had already won it once, and been twice runner-up in the previous three years.

The venue for the title was The Australian Golf Club in Sydney, and its Kensington layout was where I had stood alongside the great Jack Nicklaus as a raw rookie, just six years earlier, and topped my opening tee shot into the trees. Jack Nicklaus was going to be there again in 1982, but as it turned out I was not — except for a very painful and uncomfortable sixteen holes.

I might have played only sixteen holes of the championship, but the fact that shocked me and thousands of Australian golf fans was that Graham Marsh was not even in the country at the time the Australian Open was played.

Marsh (who is chairman of the PGA Tour) had opted to fulfil an obligation to play in Japan at the same time as the Australian Open, and for him to ignore the most prestigious event in Australia was unforgivable in my eyes.

The controversy flared up during the National PGA title at Royal Melbourne a fortnight before the Open, when I publicly criticized Marsh for turning his back on the biggest tournament in Australia to play in Japan.

My criticism prompted Marsh to issue a carefully worded statement to the Press in which he said the Australian Golf Union understood his difficulty because of the date-clash between the Dunlop Phoenix tournament and our Open. The gentlemen of the AGU may well have 'understood' Marsh's dilemma, but they were certainly not happy about him missing the Australian Open.

In his statement Marsh did not forget to shoot a barb my way over the appearance-money issue, and said so in these terms: 'Australian golf fans are aware that in the absence of pressures of this type I will continue to play in Australia without making appearance-money demands, an attitude which Greg does not hold despite his professed concern for the fans and Australian golf ....'

Certainly I had sought appearance money, but by the same token I had not pressed the issue. Marsh's decision to put his Japanese commitment higher on his priority list than the Australian Open to me smacked of hypocrisy, because he has talked often of how Australian players should give solid support to the expanding local tournament circuit. As chairman of the Australian PGA Tour his responsibility was to play in the Australian Open.

Over the years Marsh has built a big reputation in Japan, where he has campaigned very successfully, and where he is a contracted Dunlop player. No doubt there was pressure on him from his Japanese employers to compete there,

and it was the sort of pressure he could not fight.

On the Tuesday before the Australian Open was due to start I played a practice round at Kensington, and by the time I returned to my hotel in Sydney I was in agony. Laura took one look at me and immediately telephoned the hotel doctor. I was doubled up with pain, excruciating pain, and instead of attending the lavish dinner organized by the AGU for the tournament sponsors I spent the night in the Masonic Hospital.

Billy Longmuir, a long-standing friend of mine from the European tour, was in Sydney for the tournament, and we had arranged earlier in the day for him to call by for a drink before we both attended the union's function, to be held in the hotel in which Laura and I were staying. When Laura showed him into our room he must have thought he had entered a casualty-clearing station. Once the doctor had made the necessary arrangements with the hospital it was Billy who drove me there, and helped Laura settle me in.

My trouble was diagnosed as a kidney stone, and early on the Wednesday morning, the day before the tournament started, it was removed in a painful and delicate operation which left me weak and exhausted. When I came out of the anaesthetic my first reaction was to declare myself a non-starter the following day, but then I decided to delay the announcement in the hope that I might recuperate quickly enough to play.

I was discharged from hospital on the opening day of the tournament as the early starters were already teeing off. Fortunately, I had been given a late draw, and about two hours before I was due to hit off I told the tournament organizer Mr Tony Charlton that I would take my place in the field. In retrospect, it was a mistake. Perhaps if the weather had not been so boisterous I might have survived the first round and emerged with a reasonable score, but when I was 11 over par after 16 holes, and every shot required more energy than I could muster, I was forced to give up.

In fact, I had started the round with birdies at the first two holes, but not even a cushion like that could help me through. My caddie Peter Coleman carried a shooting-stick in our bag, and I sat down at every opportunity.

Toward the end of those agonizing sixteen holes I found it difficult just to focus on the ball, and my doctor was to tell me later that he had watched my progress on television, and could see that I was on rubbery legs. How right he was!

It was a dreadful disappointment. My parents had driven down from Brisbane to watch me play, and I really believed I had a great chance of winning.

Laura and I returned to Queensland the next day and I sat in front of the television set and watched my good friend Bob Shearer win his first Australian Open, finishing four shots clear of the field. I telephoned him in Melbourne the day after the tournament finished to congratulate him.

While I was playing on one side of the world I was keeping a close check on what was happening on the other side, in Europe. Weeks earlier I had competed in the Bob Hope Classic at Moor Park and played quite poorly, but victories earlier in the year, and several other high finishes, had given me a handy lead on the Official Money List. To top that order was tremendously important to me, but as the Moor Park event was my last in Europe for the year I knew that I was a vulnerable target for both Sandy Lyle and Sam Torrance, who had four more tournaments to play and would be making an all-out effort to catch me.

Opposite
I lasted just sixteen holes in the first round of the 1982 Australian Open at The Australian Golf Club, Sydney. I was still groggy from anaesthetic as this picture shows.

155

In the final analysis Lyle had to win the Portuguese Open at Penina to edge me out, but when one round of that event was abandoned with Sandy well down the order I had managed to hold them both at bay.

My European earnings for the year were £66,405.71, or just over $115.000.

Topping the Official Money List is an achievement of which I feel enormously proud, because out of the twenty-seven tournaments on the European tour which counted I competed in only eleven, and in one of those (the Scandinavian Open) I did not make the halfway cut.

In a year which embraced more than its fair share of personal trauma, and which involved many significant personal and business decisions, it was doubly rewarding. I believe my performance on the golf-course fully justified the changes of direction I had made in my career.

Topping the Official Money List also won for me the Harry Vardon Trophy, and every golfer will understand the significance of having one's name linked with the immortal Vardon.

I am also the first Australian since the great Norman Von Nida (who won the trophy in 1947) to have been successful, and as Norman has been of enormous assistance to me over the years I feel even more grateful. Besides, we are both Queenslanders!

In the seven years I have been a professional golfer I have spent more time playing in Britain than anywhere else in the world, and it has been a richly rewarding experience. The bulk of my income in those years has come from the European tour, and I like to believe that I have made some contribution to the success of the professional circuit in that part of the world.

However, professional golf in the British Isles still suffers from hang-ups that do not exist in other countries. The players and their problems are not understood to anything like the degree they are in say America or Australia, where the competitor is made to feel welcome, and club facilities are at his disposal during a tournament. It disturbs me that many English clubs do not even bother to make a change locker available for competitors, and in the UK it is unheard of for players to enjoy the peace and solitude of their own 'players' lounge', a feature at many American events. I have many times been in the position where I have had to change into my golf shoes in the club's car-park because of the lack of proper amenities at British tournament venues.

These observations may seem trivial, but for the players who provide the action which entertains millions of television viewers and countless thousands of gallery fans the lack of these important trimmings is an irritation.

Although most of my tournament golf will be played in America from now on, I sincerely hope that the friendships I have forged in Britain will remain with me always.

With Laura and Morgan Leigh, I will be back in the UK many more times to play golf.

I love it.

Opposite
You need 'body language' in this golf game. Holing a 30-footer for an eagle 3 at the long 14th on the way to winning the 1983 Australian Masters title.

157

1983 certainly looks
promising. After my
Australian Masters victory
in February, I win the
Hong Kong Open in the
same month for the
second time in four years.

My Major Victories

Year	Tournament	Country
1976	West Lakes Classic	Australia
1977	Kuzaha Open	Japan
	Martini International	Scotland
1978	Festival of Sydney Open	Australia
	Lakes Open	Australia
	Traralgon Classic	Australia
	South Seas Classic	Fiji
	New South Wales Open	Australia
1979	Hong Kong Open	Hong Kong
	Martini International	England
	Traralgon Classic	Australia
1980	French Open	France
	Scandinavian Enterprise Open	Sweden
	Suntory World Match Play Championship	England
	Australian Open	Australia
1981	Australian Masters	Australia
	Martini International	England
	Dunlop Masters	England
1982	Dunlop Masters	Wales
	State Express Classic	England
	Benson and Hedges International Open	England
1983	Australian Masters	Australia
	Hong Kong Open	Hong Kong

Acknowledgments

The publishers and the author wish to thank the
following sources for permission to reproduce the
photographs on the following pages:
Phil Sheldon 1, 2, 6, 7, 65, 66, 83, 94, 98, 103, 105, 106,
126, 132, 141, 146, 147, 149; Associated Press 13, 87, 158;
Peter Dazeley Photography 11, 80, 90, 101, 127, 130, 133;
Australian Golf Magazine 117; Colorsport 85, 88;
All Sport 89; The Herald, Melbourne 8, 12, 18, 39, 156;
Ken Rainsbury 112.
Photographs not acknowledged above were supplied by
the author.